Introduction

After some thirty-five years teaching the game of golf I am convinced that trying to learn to play golf or improve a golf swing has become much too complicated for the average human being. Most golfers, beginner and experienced players alike would rather just go play than practice and do not want or need a bunch of irrelevant "swing thoughts" swirling through their heads every time they step up to hit a golf ball.

Sure it is necessary to learn how to hold the golf club somewhat correctly and how to stand up to the golf ball to get the best results but after that I feel that the emphasis should be on just swinging the golf club toward a target and allowing the body to go along with it. In this book I have tried to make each subject clear and to the point in as few words as possible and have used great care not to make any statements that I could not demonstrate to be correct. As it is sometimes difficult to explain in writing how various movements and positions should look I have included several photos to help the reader understand my reasoning.

Every instructor has his or her own way of teaching and my feeling is that if it works don't change it. I have known for some time that I didn't teach quite the same as other instructors. I could not relate to the ideas in many instruction articles and books and really didn't like the fast talking guys on TV. All their talk and diagrams on "swing plane," "spine angle" and memorized body and golf club positions left me wondering what I had just seen. It bothers me that if I can't understand what these guys are saying or what point they were trying to get across after teaching and studying the golf swing for over thirty-five years how can anyone else? I get tired of some pitchman trying to show that the golf club must follow some "swing plan," the arms another, the shoulders another and so on. What is the point?

i

A lot of those angles and body positions might be present when we watch the great golf swings of Tiger, Rory or Luke on TV but the "experts" seem to be at a loss to explain how Jim Furyk, Bubba Watson or Tommy "Two Gloves" Gainey can possibly hit a fairway or green when those "swing planes" or body movements seem to be at odds with what is supposed to be "correct." All these players do have some things in common which is never pointed out. They all swing their golf club toward a target, have the ability to visualize the flight of their golf ball and usually know where their golf club is during their golf swings.

If you were to ask nearly any golfer about to hit their drive on the first tee at your course what they were thinking, you would get a list of five or more "swing thoughts" all to be accomplished during those three seconds or less it takes to complete a golf swing. None of these golfers would say that they were simply trying to swing their driver toward the fairway yet that would seem to be the objective. If that group on the tee happened to be made up of eight to ten-year old kids you would get entirely different answers. Most of this group would just describe what they wanted their golf ball to do; start toward the bunker on the right with a little draw or just hit a straight ball down the middle and so on. Golf is simple at that age but as we get older, read more golf articles, take more golf lessons and watch those "experts" on TV break down every golf swing into dozens of parts, the golf swing soon gets overly detailed and complicated. It also ceases to be fun.

Much golf instruction today is body-focused and is based on the premise that is if the student memorizes certain body positions and moves various body parts correctly the golf ball would somehow be propelled toward a target. When the direction of the golf ball is off or lacking in proper distance the fault must have been an incorrect movement of one or more body parts.

I will admit I taught this way for over twenty years before moving to Los Cabos, Mexico in 1996 to be the Director of Instruction at Cabo Del Sol. Knowing what I now know, if anyone ever improved their golf game before that time it would have been in spite of my teaching not because of it.

My students at Cabo Del Sol were mostly tourists only in the area for a few days so thankfully there just wasn't time to work on those memorized body and golf club positions I had always been told were necessary to have a descent golf swing. I was soon forced to abandon those old ideas in favor of having my students work more on rhythm, balance, reducing tension and trying to feel where their golf club was throughout their golf swing. I knew that the old basics like grip, stance and alignment might need some coaching but explaining how each of these factors contributed to an efficient golf swing became more important and effective than the correction itself. I knew that the body still had to do its part in an effective golf swing but mostly all it needed to do was "get out of the way" of the golf club as it was swung toward a target. Results were immediate and many of my students actually developed very good golf swings after only one or two lessons. I found that I liked to teach for the first time in my career and instead of dreading a lesson with a new student began to look forward to it.

Shortly after returning to the U. S. in 2004 to teach at La Quinta Country Club in California I read the book "Swing the Clubhead" written some ninety years ago by the great teacher Earnest Jones. I was amazed to discover that I had been using some of the same phrases in my teaching in Mexico that Jones used in his book. This summer I read Manuel de la Torre's book "Understanding the Golf Swing" and soon realized that I had switched from body-focused teaching to club-focused teaching fifteen years ago without realizing it. I knew Manuel personally when I was the Head Professional at Kenosha Country Club in Wisconsin. Manuel was the Head Professional at

Milwaukee Country Club and we teamed up in the Nelthorp Cup matches which had the top pros in Wisconsin play against the top amateurs. I also played with Manuel in the Wisconsin Open and knew him to be a top teacher and good player but had never taken the time to read his very detailed book.

I realize that many good instructors have had success with body-focused methods and there are many good golfers who are able to train the "big muscles" of the body to play a predominant part in their golf swings. I would never ask those instructors to abandon what works well for their students or those golfers having success to abandon what works for them. I just know what works best for the majority my students.

I would never claim to have all the answers and there are exceptions to every rule but I am now more convinced than ever that the most important job of the instructor is to help the student learn to react to the swinging motion of the golf club as initiated by the arms from the backswing to the finish.

I realize that this less complicated way of teaching may be hard to accept by golfers who have spent so much time and money trying to train their bodies to initiate their backswing, downswing and finish, hoping that these body-focused ideas would produce an effective golf swing. To those golfers I can only say; "I am sorry I didn't have the chance to work with you sooner."

My objective in writing this book is to have authored the most simple, logical and easy to understand golf instruction book ever written. I hope my students and readers will say I have accomplished this goal.

To the Student

This book is dedicated to all those students who have taken notes after a lesson on old scorecards, cocktail napkins or the back of a business card. You will never learn to play golf by reading a book; in fact, most of the golf instruction books I have read paint a very confusing picture of what the golf swing is all about and are overly complex. My purpose is to simplify, not complicate the golf swing.

The idea of simply training the body to react and respond to the "swinging motion" of the golf club will be dismissed by many as just too simple. After all, golf is not supposed to be simple.

Sure it is necessary to learn to hold the golf club properly, line up toward a target and have reasonably athletic posture but after that there should be no need for conscious thought of where certain body parts are as the golf club is swung back and through toward a fairway or green.

"Club-focused" teaching is not new and was taught by the great teacher, Earnest Jones, a century ago and more recently by Jim Fleck and Manuel de la Torre. In this book, Thought Reduction Golf, I have attempted to adapt the ideas of these great teachers and combine them with what I have found to be successful in my own teaching.

Part One deals with the basics of grip, stance and posture which are the same regardless of teaching philosophy then continues on to describe how to train the body to react to the "swinging motion" of the golf club from backswing to finish with as little conscious thought as possible.

Part Two describes various "short game" techniques that are necessary to learn and practice if the student expects to be able to score well regardless of swing philosophy.

I hope you will enjoy and benefit from this book and learn to play better while thinking less.

Acknowledgments

I have been writing articles for over twenty years for various publications in the United States and Mexico such as DISCOVER Los Cabos, LOS CABOS Magazine and the Gringo Gazette in Cabo San Lucas, The Plumas County News in northern California, GOLF News in the Coachella Valley and for La Quinta Country Club's Roadrunner. I thought it would be simple just to get together the ideas from those articles, add a few new ones and come up with a good golf instruction book. Well, I started this book about two years ago and after many rewrites have finally, with the help of a lot of people, put something together that I think might be fairly interesting reading and possibly even help a golfer or two with their golf swings.

I would like to thank my wife, Dale for her input, criticism and censorship; my daughter, Nico, for her photography and encouragement, Christine Regenberg for her photography and Jack Solis, Andrew Morrison and Eric Cronin for allowing me to use their fine golf swings for my photographs. Most of all I would like to thank Lisa Woodcock for her patience and for putting the pages and photos together so they would make some sense.

Thanks also to La Quinta Country Club for allowing me to use their great golf course and practice facilities for the pictures in this book. I owe a lot of thanks also to my students at La Quinta Country Club and from VIP Golf Academy who have patiently allowed me to work with them over the years.

Jack Gibson
jackg@pga.com

Contents

Part One: Golf Swing Basics

Chapter One: Two Ways To Learn The Game

Chapter Two: Three "Musts" At Address

Chapter Three: Three Critical Movements

Chapter Four: The Start Of The Swinging Motion

Chapter Five: The Downswing - A Continuation Of The Swinging Motion

Part Two: The Short Game

Chapter Eight: The Scoring Shots

In Conclusion

Part One

Golf Swing Basics

Two Ways to Learn the Game

"Body Focused" Or "Club-Focused" Learning

Much golf instruction today is *body-focused* or based on the premise that the student will be able to hit their golf ball toward a target if the positions and movements of certain parts of their anatomy are correct at various stages of the golf swing. Another premise and the one I prefer is *club-focused* which is based on understanding how the golf club should move during the golf swing and how to train the body to *react* to the *swinging motion* of the golf club.

For many students *body-focused* instruction may be fine but from my experience *club-focused* instruction gets results faster and with less thought. In order to produce a good and efficient golf swing there are basic hand, arm and body positions that may need to be corrected before even starting the golf swing. These are the same regardless of which type of instruction you would like to pursue and will be covered in detail later in this book.

How many swing thoughts do you have?

Too Many "Swing Thoughts"

For many students who have been taught that the big muscles of the body initiate the golf swing from backswing to finish, learning how to allow their body to just follow the swinging action of their golf club may seem too simple. This element requires no conscious thought what so ever when the student is about eight-years old. If you watch nearly any kid take a golf swing after they have learned to make contact you will notice that there is no thought or hesitation about just swinging their golf club toward their target.

More mature golfers insist on trying to break down what should be the very simple act of just swinging a golf club into dozens of pieces and thoughts and, unfortunately, there is always someone there to help them do it.

There should be no doubt that over-thinking and the idea that it is necessary to consciously think about so many things prior to and during a golf swing is a major factor in slow play, poor play, lack of enjoyment and intimidation of so many new or potential golfers that many never continue with the game after their first lesson. I recently asked the wife of one of our members who I had seen on the practice tee with her husband why she wasn't playing on such a beautiful day. She replied that her husband had tried to show her a few things but there was so much to remember she just wasn't ready. I am afraid this is a typical response when well-meaning husbands try to get their wives interested in the game. I am also afraid this is typical when beginners start out by taking lessons at their local driving range, retail golf store or from instructors who have not bothered to look beyond their overly detailed body-focused training.

I believe firmly that all students, beginners and more experienced players alike, need to focus on making solid contact with the golf ball using their hands and arms before being concerned that their bodies need to be in such and such a position or a "swing plane" needs to be changed in order have an effective golf swing.

It is a fact that the growth of the wonderful game of golf has slowed. We can point to the time it takes to play a round but also should be concerned about making the game too difficult to learn for the average person.

Live With The Swing You Came With

While most instructors admit that their students are trying to think about too many things when trying to hit a golf ball, they seem to find it hard to resist adding something new or different for their students to work on with every golf lesson. The instructor is not entirely to blame as most students expect to pick up some new and magical piece of advice with every session that will suddenly improve their golf game especially when they are paying in excess of $100 an hour.

It would be rare for an instructor to say to their student, *"Look, I have told you that your grip has to be changed for two months now and have showed you why it won't work the way you are doing it. You either don't believe me or are too stubborn to work on it. When you make that change, call me."* You could never imagine how many times I have wanted to say something like that or how many times I have come close. An established teacher with a sound reputation for success, a little money in the bank and nearing retirement might get away with such an overly honest comment. I will admit that I have made a few comments that have cost me the loss of a student but can you imagine how long a young Assistant would keep his or her job if they did the same?

It is a fact and something most instructors will privately agree with, that very few students will ever make any meaningful change in their golf swings regardless of how much they practice, how many golf lessons they take or how long they have been trying to make a change. This is not the fault of the student or the teacher but rather the system which insists that numerous body or golf club positions need to be "correct" if a player wants to learn the game or improve on the game they have.

A serious player can, with a lot of dedication, good instruction and a lot of meaningful practice, improve their grip, stance, alignment, timing or technique and develop a better understanding of the golf swing. With these simple improvements nearly any half-way coordinated individual can learn to play better golf.

What most players can seldom do is make any meaningful change in their basic golf swing any more than they can change the way they walk from the way they walked a year ago or ten years ago or twenty years ago.

The Tendency To Over Analyze

Our natural desire to analyze, dissect and seek to improve on everything we do and often overthink something which should be natural has caused the golf swing to become practically unteachable.

We have been taught to believe that if a top player seems to have a certain position or movement of their body or golf club at a certain stage of their golf swing that position must be the reason for their success. A slow-motion video of a Tiger Wood's golf swing might contain dozens of "correct" movements or positions that the commentators on TV claim had been the cause of his perfectly hit golf shot. On the other hand a small deviation in Tiger's body or golf club position at some point in his golf swing will be blamed for any poor shot he may happen to hit.

These observations and dissections of good player's golf swings over the years by commentators, teachers and other players have resulted in hundreds of ideas on what must be "correct." It is no wonder then that after being bombarded with so many "swing thoughts" for at least a hundred years the average golfer doesn't know what to believe, what to practice or what to just forget.

Having a mental picture of a good golf swing as a "swinging motion" from start to finish is a positive thought but trying to break that movement down into dozens of parts on every golf swing just doesn't work.

By understanding, through modern technology, so much about how the golf swing works and why it sometimes doesn't work we tend to over analyze every little position or movement. Sure you can teach a robot to play chess but does every golfer need to have exactly the same golf swing to play well? I wonder what ever happened to timing, rhythm, feel of the club head and imagination. Technology is great but what we may forget is that we are dealing with human beings and the last time I checked there was not a single robot on the membership roster of my club or signing up for my golf school classes.

Ask Before Making A Change

Your instructor may have found a position or movement in your golf swing that is making it impossible or unlikely that you can make an effective golf swing until that particular flaw is eliminated. This is sometimes the case so if that instructor can show you why a change is needed and if both you and he or she believes a change is possible go for it. I feel it is important before going further however to ask that instructor if they are primarily *body-focused* or *club-focused* in their teaching. *Club-focused* instruction would work toward allowing the swinging motion of the golf club to eliminate most flaws where *body-focused* instruction may seek to substitute your incorrect position or flaw with other memorized positions or movements and possibly just adding another thought to the process.

Weird Thoughts You Will Hear

As if we didn't have enough to think about, there have been some really weird ideas to add to our thought process in golf articles recently. I never understood what was meant by; "hands lie inside the left shoulder", "right elbow behind left hip", "golf shaft should dissect the shoulder blade" or "the pelvis, thorax and arms must fire in sequence." To me these terms sound more like a Coroner describing an autopsy on a guy who fell off a thirty story building than a golf swing.

"... and it looks like the golf shaft has dissected his shoulder blade."

Thorax, really! I had an aunt who broke her pelvis in a car accident, but thorax? This is an example of a golf instructor trying to impress a student with his medical knowledge and does nothing for learning to swing a golf club. The next time I see a student with a "chicken wing" I might just tell him to keep the golf club close to his gizzard.

Of course the one sage bit of advice we hear constantly is the idea of "delaying the hit." I wouldn't want to buy a house on the right side of a fairway at a golf course where players were trying to "delay their hit." I will talk about this later but the act of trying not to "release" the club head should be left to Professionals. For the average golfer this normally will only produce a slice or shank.

> **Not allowing a "release" of the club head due to misunderstanding of the fundamental or tightness in the wrists and hands might be the #1 flaw I see with most students and is without a doubt the number one problem with all slicers.**

I recall a member at a club where I worked in Texas who read an article promoting "delaying the hit" and ending up shanking his irons so badly he had to stop using them altogether. He ended up having so many woods of all imaginable lofts that his golf bag looked like a head cover display. He gave up chipping completely and would use his putter from fifty yards out. The Head Professional who he had been taking lessons from previously had a standing order that if anyone working in the pro shop saw this member coming toward the door they would alert him so he could hide in the store room until he had left. I don't know what ever happened to the gentleman but I am glad he had never asked me to help him while I worked there.

Forget "Swing Plane"

I don't know when the term "swing plane" became so ingrained in golf instruction but from my perspective I wish it had never been mentioned. I guess we can blame Ben Hogan for this one as there was a diagram in one of his books showing his head sticking through a plane of glass as he swung a golf club. The idea was that the golf club should follow the slant of the glass plane back on the backswing and follow the same path on the forward swing. Some golf instructor or writer started using this idea to show what a "correct" golf swing should look like. This became a "swing plane" and ever since that unfortunate moment in golf history we have been bombarded on TV and in countless articles with those words.

Having watched Hogan play and practice for hours when I was an Assistant at Colonial in Fort Worth I can tell you that he may have been able to swing back along his "swing plane" on his backswing but dropped the golf club so much down and flat on his downswing that he wouldn't even come close to that pane of glass. We now call this a "two plane swing." I can honestly say that in my thirty-some years of teaching I can't remember ever using the term "swing plane" when giving a golf lesson and probably never will unless asked to explain what it means or more importantly why not to worry about it.

CHAPTER TWO

Three "Musts" At Address

Don't Ignore the Basics

Regardless of whether you are working on letting your golf club guide your body through your golf swing or believe your body should guide your golf club there are three basics which need to be considered before even commencing your golf swing. You probably have heard or been shown all three of these "musts" before and possibly ignored them because they were just too simple and not as much fun as just taking a swing and hoping everything would work out. If the three basics of grip, posture and alignment have been ignored compensations must be made during the golf swing.

"Must" #1: The Grip

No one can deny that the hands are the only parts of the anatomy that are in contact with the golf club at address and during the golf swing. The hands and arms control the golf swing from start to finish providing both distance and power although some proponents of body-position teaching would have us believe that the body controls the swing.

An improper grip will make it practically impossible to swing the golf club effectively on the backswing or to allow the club head to square itself up when it reaches the golf ball.

I have always been puzzled as to why so very few golfers even come close to having good grips and many of those who do are holding on so tightly they have little chance of supplying any power to their golf swings. An effective grip may not be exactly the same for every player as no two individuals have exactly the same size hand, length of fingers or even the same diameter of grip on their golf club. I would suggest that anyone considering buying a new set of golf clubs or even hoping to improve their golf game let their local Golf Professional check their clubs for correct size grips.

For an experienced player making a grip change is without a doubt the most difficult change to make. We all have become accustomed to holding the golf club a certain way and there is something in the mind that resists a change however tiny that change may be. I have found that most students who are able and willing to make a change will do so right up until they start their backswing and then unconsciously revert to their old and more comfortable grip. It may take an entire one-hour lesson to eventually change a grip position even the slightest amount and it takes a very determined and very convinced player to take their new grip to the golf course. Nine out of ten times the same lesson will have to be repeated the next week.

Probably the worst advice and one reason for the usual comment, "That doesn't feel good" is the old saying that the top of the golf club should lie "diagonally" across the left hand. While this may be true to some extent, trying to consciously place the golf club in the left hand this way does more harm than good and is the reason most students have such a problem with the left hand grip. Every instructor has their own way to try to get the student to grip the golf club properly and I am no exception. As gripping the golf club properly can't easily be described in words alone, I have included some photos which will show what I feel is the easiest way to go about this.

As these photos and descriptions are very basic, some students may want to just go on to the next chapter but I would encourage even the most experienced golfer to at least take a look. Your grip might not be as perfect as you believe.

The golf club has to be held in a way that would allow the wrists to hinge naturally on the backswing and still allow the club head to be returned as close as possible to where it started as it is swung toward the target on the downswing.

If the golf club is held lightly in the fingers and the wrists remain flexible both of these will happen automatically. If the golf club is held like a rope when playing tug-of-war nothing good will happen.

One very common problem with beginners and many ladies is the "weak" left hand position combined with a "strong" right hand position as shown in the photo on the next page. In this position the right hand is trying to hinge as the club starts back but is being prevented from doing so by the left hand.

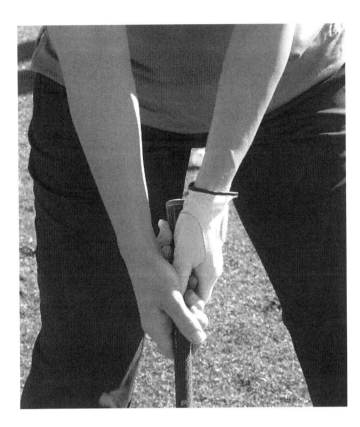

Common "weak" left hand position combined with a "strong" right hand position.

If the club face were to always return exactly to the position it was in at the address position every drive would end up in the center of the fairway and every approach shot would hit the flagstick so there is always some variation even with the best golf swing. The less you practice the greater the variation and the more you practice the less the variation.

For the majority of golfers there are four checkpoints to be remembered for a normal grip position of the left hand.

1. **The "V" formed by the thumb and forefinger should point at the right shoulder.**
2. **The emblem on the back of the glove should be entirely visible.**
3. **Your thumb should be slightly on the side of the grip.**
4. **Two knuckles should be easily visible.**

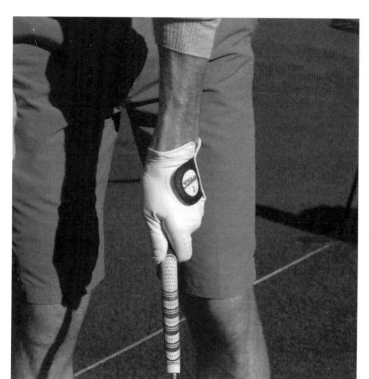

Normal left hand position with "V" formed by thumb and forefinger pointed at right shoulder.

The *weak* position with both hands as shown in the photo will produce a weak shot, high and pushed to the right or a slice for most players. Unfortunately many students have been told that the back of the left hand should face the target and the back of the right hand should face the opposite direction. This might be true when gripping the putter but not for any other golf club. This palm to palm position would place the hands on the golf club in a weak position and should be reserved for very strong players who have such fast club head speed they would tend to close their club face sooner than the average player resulting in too much hook. For everyone else a neutral grip is best.

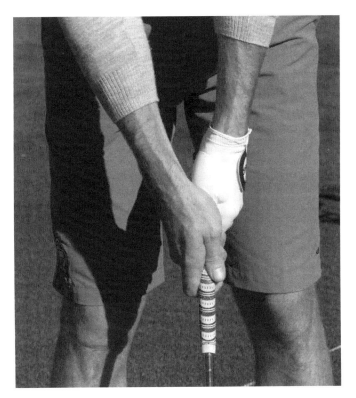

"Weak" grip with both hands.

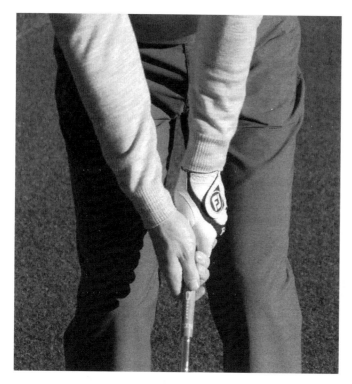

"Neutral" grip
with both hands.

You will often hear that the golf club should be gripped firmly with the last three fingers of the left hand. The problem here lies with what the student interprets as "firmly." Too firm a grip will restrict the natural hinging action of the left wrist as well as the "release" of the club head through the hitting area. Too loose a grip may cause the fingers of the left hand to "open" at the top of the backswing although the usual cause of this is a lack of wrist hinge. It is up to each student to experiment with their grip pressure to determine for themselves just how firmly to hold their golf club.

It is important to remember that the tighter the grip the less freedom there will be in the wrists throughout the golf swing.

For most of us who are right-handed the feel of where the golf club is at address or during the golf swing comes from the feeling in the fingers of the right hand. You will hear that the right hand should do nothing during the golf swing and is "just along for the ride." It is true that different good players have vastly different feelings as to just what their right hand is doing as they swing the golf club and if what they are feeling is resulting in an effective golf swing there would be no reason to change. Most would agree, however that the position of the right hand on the golf club is critical to get the golf club head square at impact with the golf ball.

As with the left hand, the position of the fingers of the right hand on the golf club need to be in a position that will allow a full hinging of the wrists on the backswing and promote a return to a square position when the club head meets the golf ball.

The right hand position has to be in agreement with the position of the left hand in order for the wrists to easily hinge in the same direction.

In other words, if the grip of the left hand is in a "weak" position, the right hand must also be in a "weak" position in order for the wrists both to be able to easily hinge in the same direction. Likewise, if the left hand is in a "strong" position the right hand should also be in a "strong" position.

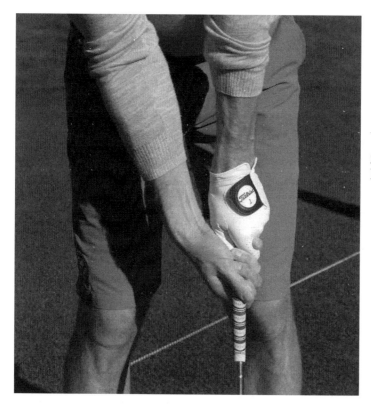

Very "strong" grip with both hands.

If the hands are in conflicting positions on the golf club, such as the two "V"s pointed at different shoulders, there is no way to determine which hand will win out by the time the golf club head gets to the golf ball and no way to determine where the golf ball will go.

For most golfers a fairly neutral grip with both hands will allow the head of the golf club to return to a fairly square position as the arms rotate through the hitting area. Just how often and effectively this happens will depend on the time spent on the practice tee trying to repeat the proper movements with a grip suited to the individual.

Presuming the left thumb is slightly on the side of the golf club, the palm of the right hand should fit over that thumb. The handle of the golf club should be gripped in the *middle* of the fingers leaving the right index finger in a "trigger finger" position. For an *overlapping grip* the little finger should lap over the index finger of the left hand. For an *interlocking grip* the little finger is place between the index and middle finger of the left hand. For juniors or people with very small hands there does not need to be any overlapping or interlocking. This is called a *ten-finger grip*.

For a neutral grip the "V" formed by the thumb and forefinger of the right hand should point somewhere between the right shoulder and the chin. This position depends on the size of the hand and length of the fingers. Most new students and many experienced players tend to grip the golf club too tightly and too much in the palm of the right hand. A good instructor can be of enormous help in determining what grip position and grip pressure is best for each golfer.

"Must" # 2: Posture

The first thing which must be understood is that not everyone can have what we, as instructors, would consider perfect posture. Not everyone stands or walks the same and no two golfers have the same posture. There are some positions I will discuss and show in the photos that either make it easier or more difficult to turn the shoulders and hips when the golf club transmits the signal.

Good Posture – Straight back, hips out, knees relaxed. The straighter the back, the easier it is to turn on the backswing.

This "hunched over" position with excessive knee bend makes it nearly impossible to swing the golf club back correctly.

The more the spine is curved or "slouched-over" the more difficult it is to turn. We often hear the term "athletic position" when describing good posture when addressing the golf ball. What is meant by this may be best understood if we watch a good tennis player waiting for a serve. They are not settled back on their heels but are set to move quickly when needed and they are not in a "slouched-over" position with their shoulders. The same would apply when addressing the golf ball to a great extent.

One bad bit of advice I hear when spouses or parents are trying to help is the old phrase, "Bend your knees." I would much rather they say, "Bend from the hips." I have found that much of the time the "slouched-over" position comes from too much knee bend and hardly any bend from anything other than the shoulders. It is true that the knees don't want to be locked but neither do they need to be bent very much. In the photos I show the "slouched-over" position as well as a comfortable and effective position which allows the spine to just turn as the golf club pulls it around. The extreme "sway back" position you see with some of the players on the LPGA Tour would be impossible to imitate for most of us so don't try it.

"Must" # 3: Alignment

In the chapter on *Starting the Backswing* we show how the golf club needs to be started along and slightly inside the line toward the target. How many times have we seen a player lay a golf club on the ground or hold it along their toe line to check their alignment then proceed to align their shoulders ten or more yards to the left? Sure the way the feet are aligned is important but much less so than the club head, shoulders, arms and torso.

Club head, hands, arms, shoulders, hips and feet all aligned toward target.

If we work on getting the shoulders arms and torso lined up it should be obvious that it will be easier to swing the golf club back along that line but most players seem to ignore this while they try to line up their feet.

As it is all but impossible to work on alignment alone I would strongly suggest getting help from your Pro or someone who understands alignment. You probably have noticed that many of the LPGA players have their caddy stand behind them to check their alignment before hitting their golf shot. If you don't have a caddy maybe your spouse would help you. Oh well; forget that.

I was working with a gentleman a few weeks ago who said he was "coming over the top" with all his golf shots. After watching him hit a few golf balls I noticed that he was, as he had said, hitting the golf ball left of his target. He was also hitting the golf ball almost exactly on line with where his arms and shoulders were aimed. His golf club was also starting back, not in line with his target but in line with his shoulders. As this was an experienced golfer with a low handicap he was soon able to make the alignment corrections I suggested and again started hitting his golf shots toward his target. It is easy to develop an alignment problem which might be interpreted as something else so I would suggest having someone check your alignment often on the practice tee. You might not be aimed where you thought you were.

I hate the phrase "coming over the top" as it really has no meaning other than the golf ball is going left of where the player thinks it should be going. The actual problems are either poor alignment or not swinging the golf club toward the target. The photos will give you a fairly good idea of what poor alignment looks like compared with how correct alignment looks.

Conflicting Alignment Positions

It is quite common for a player to have their feet aligned along their target line but have their shoulders aligned to the left. I have also noticed that even after correcting the shoulder alignment many students still have their arms aligned to the left. The problem here seems to be that the right shoulder is too high and the right arm too stiff.

This common poor alignment shows the feet correctly aligned toward the target but arms and shoulders aimed to the left.

I can't stress enough that in order to consistently swing the golf club along the target line the club head and all body parts; feet, knees, hips, belly, chest, shoulders and arms need to be lined up in that direction. The feet are the last thing to worry about lining up, not the first.

As I watch golfers on the practice tee or golf course daily trying to line up their golf shots I have a hard time guessing where most of them are trying to hit their golf balls. Many of these players have learned to re-route their golf clubs at different places during their golf swings to compensate for their poor alignment. It would be so much easier if they had just lined up correctly in the first place.

Golf Ball Position

Another factor which needs to be checked while working on alignment is where to place the golf ball in relation to the feet and how far to stand from the golf ball. Unfortunately there is no exact or correct position of the golf ball that works for every player, every golf club or every type of golf shot. Many good players seem to play their golf ball toward their left foot on all shots while others tend to position the golf ball differently for each golf club.

It is here that a little common sense might help. It is logical that in order to strike the golf ball with a descending blow such as with a wedge it would be necessary to play the golf ball a little back in the stance. As a driver is normally hit with more of a sweeping motion it should be obvious that the golf ball should be played a little forward in the stance.

Between the wedge and the driver there may be considerable deviation in the position of the golf ball with different golf clubs and even greater deviation among good players. Based on these differences about the best I can do here is suggest where the golf ball should be placed for the average golfer playing from a level lie with little wind. For a player with little movement of the weight to the left foot on the downswing the golf ball cannot be played as much toward the left without hitting a lot of fat or thin golf shots.

As golf ball position is different for the type of golf shot being played and it is difficult for any player to see themselves, I strongly suggest asking your Teaching Professional to help.

Generally I would recommend, as Ben Hogan explained in his book Five Lessons, the best way to position the golf ball might be to play all normal golf shots with the golf ball in a consistent position opposite the left foot with the major adjustment being the widening of the stance with the right foot. The other adjustment Hogan described was opening the stance with the feet as the golf shot became shorter. These ideas which I believe still apply today tend to position the left foot and the body in a somewhat similar position regardless of which golf club was being used.

Just how far to stand away from the golf ball is again a personal thing. Many of the young, strong players today seem to be reaching about as far as they can while still being to maintain their balance. This position with both arms extended to their maximum seems to promote a faster and stronger golf swing. Other players stand with their arms and hands close to their bodies and still manage to get out of the way of their arms and golf club on the downswing. Some of the difference here is due to the height of the player but mostly is in the way the players were trained or how their golf swings developed over the years.

I cannot stress enough that a serious student should work with a good teacher as they are trying to develop an efficient golf swing or make corrections in the one they have. Nearly all the top touring professionals, men and women, have a coach traveling with them or have an expert on call that knows their golf swing and understands their tendencies. Most club members ask their playing buddies or spouses.

Playing From Uneven Lies

One little trick that might help determine where to play the golf ball is by making a few practice swings before addressing the golf ball. On a downhill lie, for example, if your club head consistently makes contact with the turf back in your stance, as you take your practice swings, that is about where you should play the golf ball. You may find that on an extremely downhill lie your golf club head strikes the turf opposite your right toe. It should be obvious in this case that you should play your golf ball back toward that right toe.

To determine where to play your golf ball, take a couple of practice swings and notice where your club head will strike the turf, then play your golf ball in that location.

In the case of side hill lies the same logic will apply. When your golf ball is below your feet, any practice swing should show you that you should play the golf ball closer to your feet. If your golf ball is above your feet you will need to choke-down on your golf club and play your golf ball further away from your feet. In any case the golfer should not try to defy Mother Nature. Every lie cannot be perfectly level so your golf swing and placement of your golf ball must adapt to the situation.

When your golf ball is higher than your feet, choke up a little and allow for your golf ball flying left of your target.

How The Lie Effects Direction

Determining the direction of the golf ball from various uneven lies is a factor that can only be learned by practice. Unfortunately very few golfers spend enough time practicing these shots and very few practice areas have areas devoted to uneven lies. A golfer whose home course is mostly flat often will have a terrible time when suddenly having to play a hilly golf course. It would be impossible to describe how to play every uneven lie in a book but it should be helpful to mention some of the most common.

When your golf ball is higher than your feet, you should allow for a hook or pull. When your golf ball is lower than your feet, you should allow for a fade or push. When you need to play your golf ball forward in your stance, it likely will start to the left or when you need to play your golf ball back in your stance, it likely will start to the right. These are guidelines only and it is up to each individual player to experiment with various uneven lies to determine how they need to adjust.

Don't Set Yourself Up For Failure

In order to even begin to make an efficient golf swing it is critical to have a grip that works for your particular golf swing. It is equally important to stand in such a way that you are able to turn your body when the golf club tells you to do so and be aligned in such a way that the arms are able to swing the golf club back along your line and through toward your target.

Very few golfers with the exception of low handicap players or professional tour golfers do not have a serious flaw with their grip, stance or alignment but most students I see need help with all three. These three "musts" are static and can be improved on the lesson tee before even starting to swing the golf club. Moving faults are those which occur during the golf swing and are not so easily corrected.

> **Attempting to hit a golf ball toward a target before learning how to hold the golf club, how to stand and how to aim is a recipe for failure.**

A Couple Of Lining Up Tips

Tip number one: Pick an interim target. As discussed in the chapter on the downswing it is much easier to line up with something two feet or so in front of you than a target two-hundred yards away. Most bowlers try to start their bowling ball over a certain board, spot or arrow rather than aiming at a pin. There is always some different looking tuft of grass, an old divot or something that can be used as an interim target to aim over. This applies on the tee, fairway or even on the putting surface. If your normal golf shot is a hook, your aiming spot should be a few inches to the right to allow for this. If you are playing a fade the opposite would apply. Try this as part of your pre-shot routine and I will guarantee you will end up closer to your target.

Tip number two: Line up before addressing the golf ball. As the goal in lining up is to get your whole body parallel to the intended line to the target, walking up to that target line with your body already lined up would seem to be a logical approach. Most players have the habit of walking up from behind their golf ball with their entire body in an "open" position and then trying to gradually get lined up before starting their backswing. Many players, especially slicers, just never get their body square to their target line before starting their golf swing. After picking out your interim target try walking to a spot where your body is parallel to your target line before walking up to address your golf ball. This pre-shot routine would not only speed up your pace of play but also help you get lined up more consistently.

CHAPTER THREE

The Three Critical Movements

Making Conscious Thoughts Automatic

There are three critical moves which need to be learned then relegated to the unconscious in order for them to become parts of an efficient golf swing. These three movements are:

1. **Hinging of the wrists correctly on the backswing.**
2. **Rotation of the arms, right over left, on the downswing.**
3. **Getting out of your own way.**

As there is no good way to describe these very critical movements or positions in words I have included photos of each along with my suggestions on how to train effectively to make these three movements completely unconscious and automatic. With practice there will be no need to consciously think about these movements on the golf course. They will just happen.

Critical Movement # 1: Correct Hinging Of The Wrists

As every golf shot except the short putting stroke requires some hinging of the wrists on the backswing it is critical that we take a look at some of the misconceptions as well as right and wrong ways to execute this very necessary movement. One reason for having a grip slightly on the strong side with the left hand is that this position makes it easier to hinge the left wrist naturally as the golf club is swung back. Some students, especially women who have never played baseball or tennis have the tendency of breaking the left wrist backwards as shown in the photo and continuing that very uncomfortable looking position all the way to the top of the backswing.

This rather uncomfortable looking wrist bend could be used to disarm a thug with a knife. It is also a common position for beginners and many ladies who have a weak left hand grip position.

As far as I know the only good player who has had this unusual position is Dustin Johnson and he seems to be able to get away with it. This would be an example of there always being an exception to the rule but for everyone else it would make it very difficult to swing the golf club toward the target while trying to prevent the club head from closing too much or too soon. The closed position of the clubface at the top of the backswing that is the result of this wrist position must be compensated for by an extreme turning or sliding of the lower body to the left on the downswing to "stay ahead" of the closed clubface. The same would be true for those players who have a "flat wrist" position at the top although not as extreme. Whether to have a cupped or flat position of the wrists at the top of the backswing has been the subject of debate for years.

For players who learned to play in the wind the flat wrist position is normal. With this position the clubface will likely be closed at the top of the backswing.

The cupped wrist position seems to be more natural for most players and should never be changed just because some other player has had success with a flat wrist position.

Normal "cupped wrist".

Every player has a different feeling as to how their wrists hinge naturally on their backswing. For most people the normal hinging of the left wrist is as shown here.

The complete hinging of the wrists makes it possible to swing the golf club back as far as possible on the backswing without bending the left elbow. I am not advocating a "stiff" left arm as this would just cause more tension from the hand to the left shoulder. This hinging of the wrists gradually as the golf club is swung back on the backswing is not a problem for most golfers but if it has not become a natural and unconscious movement it will need to be rehearsed until it is.

Young player with normal "cupped wrist" position.

The club face is in an open position allowing for a good arm rotation through the impact area.

Although a gradual hinging of the wrists would be the ideal movement when taking a full backswing some very good players reach that hinged position earlier on their backswing. This is referred to as an "early set" of the wrists and while it is not an incorrect move is normally reserved for a shorter golf shot.

For right-handed players the hinging of the wrists should start with the right hand in control as the golf club is swung back on the backswing.

This would be especially pronounced when an early hinging is needed such as when hitting a bunker shot or other variations of short pitch shots. This will be discussed further in the chapter on the backswing.

Critical Movement #2: Rotation Of The Arms

This is another movement which should be perfectly natural for anyone who has ever swung a baseball bat unless they have been told that the baseball swing is different from a golf swing. I have heard or read that more than seventy percent of all golfers continually fight a slice or have given up and just allow for it. If this is the case it would be due to the fact that they were never taught correctly, have been the victim of some bad information or are just too stubborn to make this very simple correction.

Probably the #1 fault with most beginners is the lack of arm rotation or release of the club head. Without this absolutely necessary movement it is impossible to achieve distance or direction.

Player showing rotation of right arm over left.

This is why I have included it in my three "critical" movements. If this arm rotation is not a natural movement it just has to be rehearsed until it becomes an unconscious part of the golf swing. Everyone has heard of the release of the club head. This is what is meant.

The speed of the arms will naturally supply the centrifugal force that causes the arms to rotate, right over left. The faster the arms move the more the centrifugal force and therefore the faster the club head will move.

The problem is that most students are not taught that this is a natural movement and seem to be reluctant to allow it to happen.

It is absolutely necessary that beginning students be shown this movement before they hit even one golf ball.

An excellent drill for learning this move is simply swinging the arms with very relaxed wrists back to a point slightly past the right leg while the wrists hinge then swinging slowly back to a point about even with the left leg as the left arm rotates completely. As this happens the right hand will pass over and end up on top of the left. While doing this drill watch the clubface go from an open position to a closed position. I prefer to have my students swing as if they were going to hit a baseball rather than swinging close to the ground. A position at the finish where the right hand is still under the left would indicate that the clubface has been held open. This position is referred to as a "chicken wing" finish and is always the result of not allowing the arms to rotate.

"Chicken Wing"

Student before he started working on arm rotation.

41

For beginners or anyone who has had a slicing problem I suggest practicing this movement fifty or more times without a golf ball. The student can be their own judge as to when to increase the length of the swing but for a while they should just practice easy and short golf shots of fifty yards or so. You will eventually work up to a full golf swing but if you hit even one slice, start again with the short shots. You may feel that learning a completely new movement such as this left arm rotation is taking forever but you should ask yourself how long it took you to grow your "chicken wing."

Why Learn To Hook The Golf Ball

In a perfect world every drive would be hit straight to the middle of the fairway and every approach shot straight to the flagstick. Unfortunately none of us even the top PGA stars are able to always make that perfect golf swing where the golf club is swung on the perfect arc and the clubface is perfectly square at impact. As the rest of us are a long way from achieving that goal it would be nice to at least know if our golf ball is going to curve right or left.

> **There is no reason any golfer should not know if their golf ball is going to hook or slice, just how much depends on how many hours they commit to practice.**

I am often asked by beginners why the hook is preferred over the slice. I like to use the right to left spin of a bowling ball as one example. The hook in bowling is a stronger and more easily controlled shot which is more likely to result in a strike than a straight ball or spin to the right. In tennis the topspin is the stronger shot also spinning right to left. The hook or draw in golf is a stronger shot than the slice or fade and normally is the result of a good grip, correct alignment, flexible wrists and rotating arms. The slice spin, left to right, can be intentional but otherwise is the result of one or more flaws with grip, stance, wrist hinge or lack of arm rotation.

A big hook might be described as too much of a good thing but something that can be modified rather easily. An unintentional slice, on the other hand, is normally the result of bad movements or poor initial positions at address and can become uncontrollable. Normally the golf swing of a slicer is so far from correct it is impossible to straighten out without a very radical change in that students thinking as well as in the pattern of their golf swing. This just cannot be accomplished in a one-hour golf lesson. I will go into this further in the chapter on common mistakes and corrections.

As we are trying to train the body to forget bad movements and substitute them for entirely different ones, it is always necessary to over-correct and exaggerate those new movements until they become automatic. This involves learning to hook the golf ball before even thinking about how to hit it straight.

I was working with a gentleman in northern California I few summers ago who had been fighting a slice for at least twenty years. He spent more time in the pine trees than the local deer and had never seen the woods to the left. After about ten lessons mostly on reducing tightness in the wrists and arms he was actually able to hit a hook about half the time on the lesson tee. I told him that he needed to practice his new golf swing until he was able to hit fifty hooks in succession before he went on the golf course. If he happened to hit even one slice during those practice sessions he was to start the count over again. I would see the gentleman daily on the practice tee between lessons and he would always report to me whether he got up to thirty or forty straight hooks. Finally after two months he proudly reported that he had reached his goal of fifty straight shots without a slice and had actually been able to take his new swing to the golf course besting his former nine-hole score by eight strokes. Finding a student with that kind of determination is rare but for me as well as for him it was a great experience.

The "Swish" Drill

As a drill and also as a confirmation that there doesn't need to be a lot of conscious thought involved in swinging a golf club, I encourage my students to start this drill by swinging their golf club back and forth faster and faster and longer and longer until they are making the loudest "swish" possible on the downswing.

With this drill there should be no conscious thought about which body parts move or when but rather, a realization that the wrists are hinging naturally, the arms are rotating allowing the club head to release and the golf club is signaling the right side to "get out of the way".

Using this drill it doesn't take long for the student to realize that the loudest "swish" occurs when the hands and wrists are free from any tightness or tension. If I am working with a slicer it is also beneficial to point out where in the downswing the "swish" happens. If the wrists are stiff or the hands tight the "swish" takes place later and opposite the left leg whereas if there is no tension the "swish" is noticeably sooner. It should be obvious at this point that the "swish" is actually caused by how well the student releases the club head. A late release or late "swish" will cause the club head to stay open longer promoting a slice and the earlier release evidenced by an earlier "swish" will allow the club head to close sooner promoting a hook.

Using the swish drill.

A tremendous amount of club head speed can be attained with a short swing just by allowing the arms to rotate through the hitting area. Additional club head speed is gained by swinging the golf club using a fuller backswing. I have found that the average golfer is reluctant to use a full backswing or maximum club head speed because they seem to have an unconscious fear of not making solid contact or not hitting their golf ball toward their target. This is usually referred to as "guiding" the golf ball. When there isn't time to warm-up before starting a round of golf the "swish drill" is also an excellent way to get ready for that first tee shot.

Students who have been taught that they should memorize various body positions, movements or "swing planes" to make an effective golf swing rather than work on flexibility, timing and speed of the club head are facing a long uphill battle in trying to develop a golf swing.

Critical Movement #3: Get Out Of Your Own Way

As unusual as it may seem the third critical movement will need to be learned in reverse. With a full golf swing it is necessary to have someplace to swing to after the golf club has made contact with the golf ball. That finish position must be natural and comfortable so the player will have someplace to "unwind."

You must practice getting your right side out of the way in order for your arms to be able to swing the golf club toward the target.

You must learn and become comfortable with a correct and relaxed finish position in order for the body to "get out of the way" of the arms on the downswing with as little conscious thought as possible. The more comfortable your body becomes with that position the more likely you are to finish that way when hitting a golf ball.

If you are unsure or hesitant about where you should finish you are very likely to stop your swing before you should and have to fight to retain your balance. You will often hear the comment, "follow through" but trying to force your body to get to this position without first knowing how a good finish should feel will accomplish nothing. Unfortunately this term is over used and misunderstood.

I have never understood how some players can completely stop their golf club three or four feet past impact with their golf ball even with a driver. This is like having a car come to a complete stop from 90 mph in three feet. If I ever find this secret I'll sell to an automobile brake manufacturing company and retire the next day. The only thing I can figure out is that these players must have the tightest grip on the golf club humanly possible. I can understand the lack of a finish if you are buried under the lip of a bunker or swinging against a tree root but with nothing to stop the club head but air, I just don't get it.

For those players who have a hard time finishing their golf swing, there will need to be some training of the right knee and right foot to react to the turning motion of the hips. When this happens the weight that has started moving to the left foot will be able to continue all the way to a finish position with no strain on the back.

If you were to swing a golf club with your right foot stuck to the ground you are going to be very limited with how far your golf club will travel after striking the golf ball without hurting yourself.

If your right foot is "stuck" to the ground you are risking lower back injury as well as not being able to finish your swing.

If you try this position you will notice that there is a lot of strain in your lower back but as soon as you allow your right knee and right foot to "release" to the left the strain is immediately relieved and your weight is nearly all on the left heel. Again this is a matter of training the voluntary muscles to respond without conscious thought to the swinging motion of the golf club. This will require many repeated conscious movements without hitting a golf ball before it becomes a natural part of the golf swing.

Some players have the feeling that they can accomplish this movement by focusing on the movement of their hips and left side. There is certainly nothing wrong with this approach as long as it accomplishes the same result however, I have found that right-hand dominant players seem to have more awareness of where their right side is than they do their left.

A complete and relaxed position at the finish or "follow-through" is not just to look good. It is a necessary part of a golf swing which allows the golf club to be swung as fast as possible without any undue strain or injury to the player.

I suggest practicing this movement with a short wedge shot until it becomes second nature. Without this relaxed finish of the right side it is just impossible for the hips to complete their turn to the left. For many of those people who suffer from lower back problems they may find that they can make a complete golf swing with less pain when they allow their whole body to turn to the left. When the shoulders turn while the lower body does not you are asking for trouble.

A complete
and relaxed
position at the
finish.

As I have said many times to my students; "I want to see all
the spikes on your right shoe on your finish."

CHAPTER FOUR

The Start Of The Swinging Motion

Follow Your Club Head

The backswing is the start of the swinging motion of the golf club which will continue on to the finish of the golf swing when it is allowed to do its work. The first part is called a backswing because that is what it is, a swinging motion of the golf club commencing at the golf ball and continuing to the top of the backswing. It is not called a "back jerk" or "back pull" even though these might describe some of the golf swings I often see on the golf course and practice tee.

Starting Back

We have all heard that the backswing should be started back "in one piece" but this does not mean that the second the club head starts to move all the various body parts start to move at the same instant. As the club head obviously has further to travel along that circular path of the backswing it should start first.

I have found that for right-handed dominant players, the only way to start the club head back with any consistency is by controlling that motion with the right hand.

Just stand still.

The feeling should be that the body remains as still as possible until it receives the message from the golf club through the hands and arms that it is time to go along.

As the golf club is swung back the feeling should be that the hands and arms signal the rest of the body when it is necessary to move. As the shoulders start to rotate they signal the hips to rotate when needed and the hips send a message to the left knee that it too may join in the action. Many of the longest hitters in the game are able to rotate their shoulders 90 degrees or

53

more while their hips and legs hardly move. This lack of lower body movement makes it easier to get the weight on the left foot by the time the club head reaches the golf ball. Most players lack the flexibility to copy this position and will need to allow their hips to rotate to have any chance of taking the golf club back adequately on the backswing.

As the golf club is started back it will need to follow a slight curve in order to find its way to the top of the backswing. As no two people have the same build this slightly inside path will be different for everyone. It should be obvious that a shorter player will need to follow a greater curve than a taller player and it may take the help of a good teacher to find the correct path back.

The first motion of the golf club as it is swung back should be along the shoulder line. If the shoulder line is toward the target the first movement of the golf club should be along that line for the first few inches before starting to follow that inside curved path. For a player intending to play a fade the shoulders and arms will be lined up to the left of the target line and the natural first move of the club head will be slightly outside the normal line to the target. The club head may remain aligned to the target or opened more depending on the amount of fade or slice needed. When playing a draw the opposite would apply. The arms and shoulders would be aligned to the right and the first part of the club head's path would be inside the normal target line. The whole body should be lined up the same direction as the shoulders and arms. How much club head is closed depends on how much draw or hook is needed.

Practicing taking the club head back on a correct and consistent path according to type of golf shot planned will help the player reach a position at the top of the backswing that will make it easier to swing the golf club toward their intended line on the downswing.

Don't Be Afraid To Use Your Right Hand

I have found in thirty-five or more years teaching that many right-handed students are reluctant to use their right hand to start the golf club back even though they will admit they have more feel and control of the golf club this way. For lefties, the same thing applies. One good thing about working with kids or beginners is that they will naturally use their right hand, if right-handed, to start the golf club swinging. Unfortunately this natural feeling and advantage a new student has is often thwarted before they get to the lesson tee my a parent or friend who has cautioned them against using their right hand as something terrible would happen to them if they dared do so.

I am not advocating a sudden pickup of the club head with either hand but by using the right hand to start the swinging motion of the golf club the golfer would have more control over the path of their club head and the rhythm and length of the backswing.

By controlling the golf club with their dominant hand a player would be more likely to be able to set the golf club in the position at the top of the backswing they are trying to achieve.

There has been a lot of misinformation about what would happen if the dominant right hand were to be in control of the backswing. It would be best to just ignore these stories as they are not based on fact. I have never understood why taking the golf club back on a more consistent path, being able to control when the wrists start to hinge, being able to swing to a better position at the top of the backswing or even being able to more accurately tell where the club head is throughout the backswing are such bad things. Most teachers and students understand that it is necessary to use the right hand to "pick-up" the club head sooner when hitting from a bunker, high grass or when hitting other short golf shots without releasing some monster but in many cases want to maintain the taboo against using the right hand for anything else.

The Correct Sequence Of Events

What I have described here thus far is the proper sequence of events for a full backswing for a right-handed player.

> **The golf club starts the swinging motion under the control of the right hand, followed by the arms, shoulders, hips and legs in that order.**

The shorter the golf shot the less movement there will be as no body parts need to move until the arms and golf club have signaled them to do so. Older players may have been taught that there is a "shifting" of weight to the right foot on the backswing and then to the left on the downswing. Trying to change that thinking and substituting it for the idea of just standing still until the golf club signals the body to move is a difficult task.

Heavier players often have a more difficult job taking the golf club back far enough on their backswing without more turning or sliding of the hips than a slimmer person. This sometimes results in more weight moving back to the right foot than would be ideal on the backswing. When this less-than-ideal turning or even the shifting of the weight back to the right foot happens that player will need to work extra hard to get their weight planted on their left foot by the time the head of the golf club reaches the golf ball on their downswing. This is a matter of timing but, as some heavier folks seem to have more rhythm, is not impossible.

Clubface Position At The Top Of The Backswing

An improper grip with either hand or both hands or the improper hinging of the wrists will cause the head of the golf club to be in a *very closed or very open position* at the top of the backswing. While there can be no such thing as a "perfect" or "correct" club head position at the top an extreme position either way will result in the player needing to manipulate their golf club in various ways to have any chance of getting their club head square by the time it reaches the golf ball on the downswing.

Neutral position

Whether the club head is open, closed or square it is critical that all players, regardless of ability, know where their golf club and club head are at the top of their back swing.

There are a number of top players who have the face of their golf club partially closed at the top of their backswings but very few who have the clubface extremely open unless they are hitting from a greenside bunker or striving for extra loft on a wedge shot. A player with a *closed* clubface position at the top must slide and turn their hips sooner than normal in order to deliver their club head to a square position at impact with the golf ball. On the other hand, a player who has had a very open clubface at the top must be sure that their body doesn't move too rapidly or before the clubface has had time to square itself.

Open position

A closed clubface position at the top would be when the face of the golf club is facing up. A very open clubface position would be when the toe of the golf club is pointed down and slightly behind or away from the player. The best position for most players would be a slightly open position where the toe of the golf club is pointed straight down. There are many degrees of difference between the two extremes of open face or closed face positions depending on grip position, wrist flexibility, wrist hinge and the type of shot being executed. It will be up to each player to determine the best position for their clubface at the top of their backswing.

Very closed position

As most players are not as flexible as my models they obviously cannot achieve those body positions at the top of their backswings. Few older players are able to get the shaft of their golf club anywhere near horizontal with the ground or have the flexibility to allow their bodies to turn as much as they would like so both teacher and student will need to adapt to these limitations.

It is necessary to determine just what the "top of the backswing" is for many players and not have them attempt to turn their bodies so much that they are in a strained or uncomfortable position.

I remember the comment of a player on the Senior Tour a few years ago when asked about his very short backswing. His answer was that it really didn't matter how long his backswing was as long as he could hinge his wrists. As always, there are exceptions to the rule. Steve Stricker has less hinging of his wrists than any other top player but makes up for it by having exceptional arm strength and great timing.

I am confused that although the correct hinging of the wrists with either hand is about the same motion as used when drinking a glass of wine, many of my students have a problem doing the same thing with their golf club. No, beer drinkers; a mug has a handle and that position doesn't work.

A complete hinging of the wrists is an absolute necessity for most players regardless of age or flexibility of other body parts.

61

"Down The Line", "Across The Line" Or "Laid-Off"

These three terms refer to the direction the shaft of the golf club is pointed at the top of the backswing. "Down the line" would mean that the shaft is pointed directly at the target when the player reaches the top of the backswing. A player with a full shoulder turn and fully hinged wrists would normally come close to achieving this "desired" position and much instruction considers this something to work towards.

Golf club pointed "down the line".

An "across the line" position would mean that the shaft of the golf club is pointed to the right of the target. I would consider this position close to correct if not done in the extreme. This position requires a greater shoulder turn than normal and a "cupped wrist" position of the left wrist. An extreme "across the line" position might make it more difficult for the player to swing their golf club toward their target but attempting to change a wrist position that is normal and comfortable or trying to restrict a natural shoulder turn is nearly impossible and are corrections that will seldom hold up under pressure.

Golf club pointed "across the line".

A "laid off" position would be when the shaft of the golf club is pointed behind and away from the player. With this position the hands normally are in a much lower position (a flat position) than the player's body build and height would dictate. The golf club would tend to approach the golf ball from a much lower position as opposed to the steeper angle of attack with the other two positions. This closer-to-the-ground approach to the golf ball would make it more difficult for the player to play from higher grass and would require that the player slide their hips to the left more than normal to "get out of the way" of the arms and golf club.

Golf club in the "laid-off position".

Attempting to change other than extreme "laid off" or "across the line" positions will nearly always do more harm than good and the player would be much better off just learning to swing their golf club toward their target regardless of where their golf shaft is pointed at the top of their backswing.

The Waggle

Some preliminary movements prior to actually starting the golf swing serve as tension reducers; some are nervous habits and others are just irritating to watch. With what some call "old school" golf swings where rhythm seemed to be as important as mechanics the waggle was a necessary part of reducing tension and setting the tone for the swing itself. No two golfers have the same waggle even when their golf swings seem identical. Ben Hogan could be identified by his waggle from two hundred yards away. Hogan felt that the waggle was a necessary part of the golf swing and would never hit a golf ball before going through this step. For him the waggle helped set the tone and rhythm for his golf swing. I have seen some terrible waggles which would in no way contribute to a good golf swing and which were so different from the actual golf swing they could not be of any help. Just as a good waggle could be a prelude to a good golf swing, a bad waggle can set the tone for a poor swing. Few instructors today consider the waggle an integral part of a golf swing and it is something so individual I would not attempt to teach it unless I see that what is being used is hurting rather than helping.

The Forward Press

As an instructor I see a lot of nervous movements taking place just before the golf club is started back on the backswing. The most common and the one which seems to have the most detrimental effect is when the player closes the clubface just before starting back. This unnecessary movement has the effect of giving the player a bad mental image of the direction the golf club should be swung. This very common nervous habit causes the player to start their club head outside their intended path to the target then loop it back inside on the way back.

65

Nearly every good player has some slight movement, often hardly noticeable, to help get their golf club started back on their backswing. It could be a slight movement of the hands forward, a slight movement of a knee, a very slight movement of the head or even a light squeezing of the grip. As with the waggle, these movements are individual and have usually been developed over a long period of time. I have often suggested that a player who has a forward press that is causing a problem try substituting it for one that is less harmful but may serve the same purpose.

The Practice Swing

A practice swing like the waggle or forward press should be a rehearsal of the actual golf swing being considered. It may serve as a tension reducer, a loosening-up exercise or a sample of the real swing to come. I am not opposed to a player taking two or three practice swings before actually hitting their golf ball provide they serve some purpose but many of the practice swings I see on the golf course do nothing but waste time. As most amateurs have a problem releasing their club head, a few swings working to hear a "swish" are sometimes helpful. This also is a great drill if the player has overslept and hasn't had time to hit practice balls before going to the tee.

CHAPTER FIVE

The Downswing
A Continuation Of The Swinging Motion

Velocity, Direction And Spin

The velocity of the golf ball is determined by the speed of the club head, the trampoline effect (legal or not) built into the clubface and the amount the golf ball is compressed.

Club head speed is determined by how fast the arms are moving. The speed of the arms causes the centrifugal force which gives the club head its speed (release of the club head). Any tightness or tension in the hands or wrists will diminish that club head speed.

The initial direction of the golf ball is determined by the direction the head of the golf club is swung with the arms.

Any right or left spin of the golf ball is determined by whether the club face is open, closed or square when it reaches the golf ball. This clubface position is determined by the grip, the amount of tension in the wrists and when the natural arm rotation is allowed to happen.

Backspin is caused by the clubface striking the golf ball at a downward angle and increased by the groves on the face of the golf club and the speed of the club head. A hook or slice would have both backspin and sidespin.

67

The variations in golf ball flight discussed here may not be of great concern to the average beginner who is just trying to make solid contact with the golf ball and have it end up somewhere near their intended target. I feel it is important, however, for any player regardless of ability to at least have some knowledge of what factors in the golf swing determine distance, direction and spin of the golf ball.

I always emphasize to my students who often are overly concerned about direction or whether or not they have hit a shot with backspin to first work on solid contact. When they start hitting the golf ball consistently on the center of the clubface, we can start working on direction and spin.

By concentrating on the three critical positions of the hands and body and the three critical movements during the golf swing, discussed in earlier chapters, ball flight and being able to swing toward a green or fairway will start to come naturally.

With a proper grip and lack of tension in the wrists the club head will travel from an open position at the top of the backswing to a square position at impact and to a closed position right after impact and on to the finish of the golf swing. No manipulation of the club with the hands is required. This open to closed movement of the club head is the result of the centrifugal force or swinging motion of the golf club which can only occur when the right hand and forearm cross over the rotating left arm. This critical movement was discussed in the chapter on "Three Critical Movements." Any tightness or tension in the hands or wrists will act as impediments to this natural arm rotation resulting in loss of distance and direction. On shorter golf shots this movement may be restricted intentionally leaving the clubface square or open as will be shown in the chapter on short game shots. Here I am discussing a full golf swing only.

Different Strokes For Different Folks

For the player who has allowed much of his or her weight to move to the right (back) foot on their backswing or even outside that foot much more emphasis must be placed on moving that weight back to the left (front) foot sooner than would have been necessary if they had not moved to the right in the first place.

Players with thicker bodies may need to let more than the desired amount of weight move back to the right on their backswing in order to be able to swing their golf club back to anything resembling a full backswing. In this case I would say they should do whatever they have to do to get the golf club back.

With all efficient golf swings whether they have arm-initiated or hip-initiated downswings the club head speed, direction of the swing and the body positions are very nearly the same by the time the golf club makes contact with the golf ball. From my experience the arm-initiated downswing and just learning to swing the golf club toward the target as the hips and other body parts follow along is easier to control, requires less conscious thought and is more consistent. Different things work for different people and each student should practice whatever works best for them. Just let your instructor know what you are trying to do so you both will be "on the same page." If you are attempting to make a move that may be entirely wrong or not suited to your particular golf abilities the best place to find out is on the lesson tee.

Starting Down With Power And Control

There always seem to be some confusion and a lot of disagreement about how to best start the downswing for maximum power and control. As no two players have exactly the same position at the top of the backswing or even can agree on how they got there, it would be impossible for every player to have exactly the same feeling as to how to start the downswing. When the player's weight has remained centered all the way to the top of the backswing and the swinging motion of the golf club has initiated a full shoulder turn there should be the feeling of being "wound-up" with the upper body as with my model.

"Wound-up" position at the top.

From this ideal position it is possible to swing as hard as possible with the hands and arms toward the target. As there is very little hip rotation with a young, flexible player there is considerable tension built up as the shoulders complete their turn so at the instant the hands and arms start down that release of tension from the shoulder turn causes the hips to start their slide and turn to the left. By the time the hands have reached a point slightly ahead of where they started on the backswing the weight has become firmly planted on the feet with slightly more weight on the left.

When the arms and hands have reached their maximum speed, centrifugal force takes over and the club head is slung to the golf ball and the golf ball is sent on its way. At this point the body has moved out of the way of the arms and is pulled on to its finish position by the swinging motion of the still accelerating golf club.

If the player has worked diligently on swinging toward their target there is very little that can go wrong with the golf shot in the above scenario. Half way down on the downswing is too late to decide to make a change so to even have any thoughts of doing so is futile. With practice the only thought should be that of just swinging the head of the golf club toward the target.

The Downswing For The Rest Of Us

The ideal downswing as described above is beautiful to watch and a great thing to feel when it occasionally happens. As we are dealing with individual feelings even the best players have different ideas when talking about how they start their downswings even though their backswings and positions at the top of their backswing may be similar. Many will say they have a cue that helps them get certain body parts started while others don't give it a thought except just swinging toward a target.

71

Even with the best players there are often flaws or personal swing traits which need to be compensated for to produce a good golf shot. A player who has a "flat" wrist position at the top will need to move their body sooner and keep it moving left so the clubface will not be too "closed" at impact. Another player who lets a little more weight slide back to the right on their backswing will need to move their weight sooner to the left on their downswing to get their feet planted by the time the golf ball is struck. A slow-motion video of the top players will usually show that the arms and hips have actually started to move at the same time so it all boils down to what each individual feels is happening even when it actually isn't.

The average player regardless of how much they practice, how many golf lesson they take or what they believe they look like at the top of their backswing is often so far away from an even acceptable position that there is simply so way they can all think about starting their downswing with the same thought or movement.

Very few average players and hardly any poor players or beginners spend enough time working on the basics of grip, posture, alignment, proper wrist hinge, arm rotation and balance and hardly any work on simply learning to follow the swinging motion of the golf club or knowing where their golf club head is during their golf swing.

Not everyone can have what might be considered a good golf swing but there is no reason or excuse for any player not knowing where their golf club is or what it is doing throughout their golf swing.

Just Swing The Club Head Toward The Target

Even when there are no serious problems with their backswing and no obvious flaws with their position at the top, many players still experience problems hitting their golf ball toward a target. The most common problems are a "pull" to the left of the intended target or a "slice" which starts left and curves back to the right. A "push" to the right is a less common problem.

If the cause of these off-line shots has not been the player's inability to "get out of the way" with their lower body the only other cause would be the player's lack of feel and control of where their golf club and club head are during their golf swing.

Players who have been taught or believe that their bodies control their golf swing will try to correct these faults by attempting to change positions or movements of various body parts or trying to change their "swing planes." They may try to change the path of their golf club on their backswing, place their elbows or shoulders in different positions at the top of their backswing, start their golf club more inside or straighter back as they start their backswing and so on without showing any permanent improvement.

What these players need to realize is that the key to hitting a golf ball toward a target, regardless of where their golf club is at the top of the backswing, is simply swinging the club head toward that target.

Sure, having a perfect backswing, perfect position at the top of the backswing and perfect balance will make it a lot easier to swing that club head toward the target but these so called "perfect positions" and perfect "swing planes" will be of little help if the player continues to neglect the ultimate goal of simply swinging toward the target.

It cannot be over-stated that the hands are the only parts of the anatomy that are in contact with the golf club and it is the hands and arms which control the direction the golf club is swung regardless of the position of various body parts at the top of the backswing or how the golf club was swung back on the backswing.

Hitting It Between The "Goal Posts"

For players who would like to work on learning to swing toward a target I suggest a pair of alignment sticks set in the ground about ten or so yards ahead of the player and about four feet apart to act as "goal posts." Keeping the target and golf ball lined up between those posts should give the player a good idea of just how far off their golf ball would be sent if it is not started in the center of the two posts. When the player is able to hit their golf ball consistently between those posts they will be less likely to miss their target on the golf course.

Practicing the "Goal Post" drill.

Pick Out An Interim Target

As some of your playing partners may be bothered by your use of alignment sticks on the golf course I would suggest they be used exclusively on the practice tee. The next best thing, which I wrote about in the chapter on "alignment," is picking out some irregularity in the turf a few feet ahead of your golf ball to line up with. If you have not been able to work sufficiently with your "goal posts" on the practice tee your "spot" in the turf should be a few inches to the right of your target line just as the center of your "goal posts" will seem to be to the right of your target line on the practice tee. As in bowling, a ball rolled or hit over an interim target, will likely end up close to the final target.

Staying Behind The Golf Ball

I'm sure you have all been told to "stay behind the ball" but may have not understood just what is meant or how to go about it. This is one of those fundamentals that are very hard to describe but will be understood the first time you feel it. One reason for rotating the shoulders on the backswing is to be able to have the club head approach the golf ball from "inside" as opposed to coming from a steeper angle.

Staying behind the golf ball.

The correct feeling would be that the first movement of the hands from the top of the backswing is down toward the ground rather than toward the golf ball.

In order to teach some students to grasp the concept of starting down I have often suggested they try to hit their right foot as they start their downswing. So far I have never had a student actually hit their right foot with their golf club. By starting this way the hands and golf club will be set to follow that semi-circle into the contact area. If the first movement has been the shoulders starting to unwind the hands and golf club are set to approach the golf ball from "outside" and it will then be impossible to swing the golf club toward the target. Another way to put this which some players are able to relate to is that the golf club should approach the golf ball a little at an angle from behind the right foot.

The first movement of the downswing is toward the ground.

Should You "Keep Your Eye On The Golf Ball?"

It seems to be a natural instinct to want to watch the golf ball all the way to the target. The problem for many players is that they have developed the habit of looking toward the target before their golf club has reached the golf ball. Even worse is the habit of letting the head move forward with the eyes also before any contact with the golf ball has been made.

This young player demonstrates four very necessary parts of an effective golf swing.

1. Staying behind the ball.
2. Keeping the eyes focused on the spot where the golf ball was sitting,
3. Excellent arm rotation
4. Getting the right side out of the way

I suggest to my students to focus on where they want their club head to strike the turf rather than watching the golf ball too intently. The goal here, when practicing, is to watch for the divot when hitting irons and watch for the tee to move when practicing a tee shot. Many players have no idea where their golf tee has gone when they have hit a drive because they were just not watching long enough.

Letting the eyes and head move through to a finish position is a natural part of a well-timed golf swing and attempting to stay down past the point where the arms have signaled the head and eyes to move will prevent a natural and free finish.

I suggest doing a timing drill using a short wedge shot of fifty yards or less. For this drill take a rather full backswing but try just letting the golf club drop slowly down. Keep your head and eyes perfectly still through the hitting area and consciously let your head turn when your right arm touches your chin and no sooner. This may take fifty or so very slow and deliberate golf swings before attempting to hit a full golf shot. Old habits are hard to break but replacing the habit of "looking up" with the habit of letting the right arm control the head is a positive move.

Learning to keep the eyes and head from moving prematurely rather than waiting for the arms to tell them to move is a timing move that must be practiced diligently to have any chance of success on the golf course.

CHAPTER SIX

A Summary Of Swing Basics

Chapter One
Two Ways To Learn

- ➤ *"Body-focused" instruction is based on the premise that if the movements and positions of various body parts are "correct" at certain stages of the golf swing the golf ball will travel toward a target.*

- ➤ *"Club-focused" instruction is based on learning how the golf club should move during an efficient golf swing and how to allow the body to react to the swinging motion of that golf club.*

- ➤ *Kids are able to swing their golf club toward a target with no conscious thought but more mature golfers insist on trying to break down what should be the very simple act of just swinging a golf club into dozens of pieces and thoughts.*

- ➤ *Having a mental picture of the golf swing as a "swinging motion" is a positive thought but trying to break that movement down into pieces is just too complicated.*

- ➤ *Not allowing a "release" of the club head due to tightness or tension in the wrists or hands may be the #1 flaw with most golfers and is the case with all slicers.*

Chapter Two
Three "Musts" At Address

Must #1: The Grip

> ➤ *An improper grip will make it practically impossible to hinge the wrists correctly on the backswing or to allow the clubface to square itself up when it reaches the golf ball on the downswing.*

> ➤ *The golf club has to be held in a way that would allow the wrists to hinge naturally on the backswing and still allow the club head to be returned as close as possible to where it started as it is swung toward the target on the downswing.*

> ➤ *The tighter the grip the less freedom there will be in the wrists throughout the golf swing.*

> ➤ *Both hands must be "in agreement" with their position on the golf club. If the hands are in "conflicting" positions there is no way to determine which will win out during the golf swing and no way to predict where the golf ball will go.*

Must #2: Posture

> ➤ *Not every player can have the same posture but generally a straight back will make it easier for the spine to turn both on the backswing and downswing.*

Must #3: Alignment

> ➤ *Alignment is how the clubface, shoulders, arms and torso are aligned to a target. Lining up the feet has little to do with the direction of the golf swing.*

> ➤ *Attempting to hit a golf ball toward a target before learning how to hold the golf club, how to stand and how to aim is a recipe for failure.*

Chapter Three
Three Critical Moves During The Golf Swing

Critical Move #1: Wrist Hinge

> ➤ *Hinging of the wrists on the backswing is made possible by a correct grip and a lack of tightness or tension in the fingers and wrists.*

> ➤ *A cupped wrist position seems to be natural for most players and should never be changed just because some other player has had success with a flat position.*

> ➤ *For either right-handed or left-handed players the hinging of the wrists should start with the dominant or lower hand in control. This is contrary to much teaching.*

Critical Move #2: Rotation Of The Arms

> ➤ *Allowing the left arm to rotate as the right arm crosses over it is what is meant by a "release" of the club head. This movement may need to be*

rehearsed until it becomes completely automatic. Without this movement it is impossible to achieve distance or direction.

➤ The speed of the arms will naturally supply the centrifugal force that causes the arms to rotate, right over left without any manipulation of the golf club with the hands. The faster the arms move the more the centrifugal force and therefore the faster the club head will travel.

➤ As the topspin forehand in tennis or the hook in bowling are stronger shots, learning to hook the golf ball is absolutely necessary for any serious student of the game of golf. There is no reason any golfer should not know if their golf ball is going to hook or slice; just how much depends on how many hours they commit to practice.

➤ As nearly all ladies and many men do not have enough club head speed to achieve the distance they should be getting, I encourage using the drill of just swinging the golf club back and through until the loudest "swish" possible can be heard. With this drill there is no conscious thought about which body parts move or when but rather a realization that the wrists are hinging naturally, the arms are rotating and the golf club is signaling the body to "get out of the way."

Critical Move #3: Get Out Of Your Own Way

➤ It is critical that all students become comfortable with a correct and relaxed finish position in order for their body to be able to "get out of the way" of the hands and arms on the downswing. The more comfortable the body becomes with that position the more likely the finish will happen without any conscious thought.

➤ *In order to swing the golf club toward a target the body must respond to the swinging action of the golf club and "get out of the way" of the arms. For maximum arm speed it is necessary to practice turning the lower body to the left with just enough weight remaining on the right foot to maintain balance at the finish.*

Chapter Four
The Start Of The Swinging Motion

➤ *The feeling should be that the body remains as still as possible until it receives the message from the golf club, through the hands that is time to go along.*

➤ *A right-handed player just cannot make a consistent "one piece" start back unless the right hand is in control.*

➤ *The goal is to "swing" the club head with as little conscious thought as possible while the body responds to that club head.*

➤ *It is often necessary to retrain various body parts to do nothing until their golf club tells them to respond.*

➤ *It must be realized that any weight moved back to the right foot on the backswing will need to be returned to the left foot before the golf club reaches the golf ball on the downswing.*

➤ *As it is impossible to keep the weight on the inside of the right foot on the backswing if the player's shoe has been trained wrong it may be necessary to purchase a new pair of golf shoes.*

➢ On the backswing the golf club starts the action followed by the arms, shoulders, hips, left leg and left foot.

➢ Whether the club head is open, square or closed it is critical that all players, regardless of ability, know where their golf club and club head are at the top of the backswing.

➢ A complete hinging of the wrists is an absolute necessity for most players regardless of age or flexibility of other body parts.

➢ Due to age, build and flexibility it is necessary to determine just where the "top of the backswing" is for different players and not have them attempt to turn their bodies so much that they are in a strained or uncomfortable position

➢ Attempting to change an other than extreme "across-the-line" or "laid-off" position will nearly always do more harm than good and the player would be much better off just learning to swing their golf club toward their target regardless of where their golf club shaft is pointed at the top of their backswing.

Chapter Five
The Downswing
A Continuation Of The Swinging Motion

➢ The velocity of the golf ball is determined by the speed of the club head.

➢ The speed of the club head is determined by the speed and rotation of the arms.

➤ *The initial direction of the golf ball is determined by the direction the golf club is swung.*

➤ *Any sideways spin of the golf ball which produces a hook or slice is determined by the position of the clubface at contact with the golf ball.*

➤ *The position of the clubface at impact is determined by the grip, amount of tension in the wrists and how quickly the arm rotation occurs.*

➤ *Backspin is caused by the downward stroke of the club head, the speed of the club head and by the groves on the clubface.*

➤ *The downswing should be a continuation of the swinging motion of the golf club which started with the backswing. As the golf club is started down the arms are in control and send a signal to the hips and other body parts to join in the action. The body needs only to be trained to react to that swinging motion with as little conscious thought as possible.*

➤ *For the player who has allowed much of his or her weight to move to the right (back) foot in their backswing or even outside that foot, much more emphasis must be placed on moving that weight back to the left (front) foot sooner than would have been necessary if they had not moved so much in the first place.*

➤ *The correct feeling at the start of the downswing is that the first movement of the hands is down toward the ground rather than toward the golf ball.*

➢ *The basic cause of most golf shots being hit off-line, regardless of body or golf club positions, is simply that the player has not swung their club head toward their target.*

➢ *The hands are the only part of the anatomy that are in contact with the golf club and it is the hands that control the direction the golf club is swung regardless of the position of various body parts at the top of the backswing or how the golf club was swung back on that backswing.*

➢ *Learning to keep the eyes and the head from moving prematurely rather than waiting for the arms to tell them to move is another part of timing that has to be worked on diligently on the practice tee to have any chance of success on the golf course.*

CHAPTER SEVEN

Common Mistakes And Corrections

Focusing on the negatives of what things may have gone wrong during a golf swing to cause an errant golf shot will rarely correct any problem. Thinking of the golf swing as a swinging motion of the golf club from start to finish is a positive thought which will go a long way toward preventing an undesirable golf shot before it happens.

Any player can hit a disastrous golf shot during a round of golf and many times no logical reason can be found for doing so. In many cases that shot can be traced back to tension or a temporary loss of timing or rhythm in the golf swing. For the average player most poorly hit golf shots, if repetitive, are the result of some habit developed over a long period of time usually from a false mental image of how the golf swing should look and feel. Very few players were ever taught how to develop the mental image or feeling of just swinging the golf club while allowing the body to respond.

Most swing problems can be traced back to various body parts making wrong or unnecessary moves without being told to do so by the golf club.

Although my whole idea throughout this book has been to eliminate as many conscious thoughts as possible it is often necessary to identify and try to correct certain bad habits which make the simple act of swinging a golf club a difficult achievement. Attempting to substitute one undesirable movement or position with another memorized motion or position usually just adds to the confusion and does little for the rhythm of the golf swing. It is better and easier to work on retraining the student's various body parts to do nothing until the golf club sends them the signal that is time to move.

Just standing still until you feel a pull or signal from the golf club, hands or arms that it is time to move along would seem to be a rather simple proposition but years of moving a knee, for example, the instant the club head starts back on the backswing is not as easy to correct as it would seem. Some players develop the habit of moving their left knee too soon and others allow their right knee to slide to the right for no logical reason. This movement is normally called a "sway." Both of these movements are examples of voluntary muscles making involuntary movements due to the fact that they have been trained incorrectly. Either of these unnecessary moves will result in the player moving so much weight back to the right on the backswing that they have little chance of getting their weight back to the left foot by the time the club head reaches the golf ball on the downswing.

These very common flaws usually result in topped shots, fat shots and, as the body will seldom be able to get out of the way of the arms soon enough, an inability to swing the golf club toward the target. This inability to swing the golf club toward a target is often the major cause of a pull, slice or even a shank. Unfortunately, this rather obvious swing flaw just cannot be corrected during a one-hour lesson and probably not without the help of a patient golf instructor.

Retraining of any of the body parts that may be moving incorrectly or at the wrong time just cannot be successful without numerous hours of dedicated and supervised practice.

Most of my one-on-one golf school students, who I am able to work closely with for fifteen or more hours, show marked improvement in their ball striking as we have time to work diligently on eliminating flaws and developing more of a feel of how the body should react to the swinging motion of the golf club. The average student who takes a one-hour lesson and then goes to the golf course with their buddies usually plays worse as they are caught between their old bad habits, trying a new technique and getting other advice.

Treating The Symptom Rather Than The Cause

Eliminating The "Chicken Wing"

One thing that makes any improvement in a player's golf swing so difficult is the tendency of the player and often the instructor to try to correct some flaw in a golf swing as if it were the cause of a problem when it may only be a symptom. One very common position which shows up right after contact with the golf ball is the well-known "chicken wing" finish. In this position the left arm of the player finishes high and pointed toward the target. The left hand is also higher than the right and the clubface has remained in an open position. The ball-flight may be high and normally will slice to the right.

When I see a player attempting to correct their "chicken wing" by trying to force their left elbow to point down on their finish or try to force their arms to finish more together it is hard to resist not shouting something like; "That's not the problem. You just need to let your arms rotate through the hitting area." So far I have been able to restrain myself and keep my job.

One of the three very basic movements in a golf swing is the act of allowing the right hand and arm to rotate over the left as the face of the golf club travels from open to closed, as I explained in an earlier chapter. With this movement there can be no "chicken wing" and trying to correct this position in any other way is entirely futile.

I have found also that there sometimes is a misconception with beginners and sometimes with more experienced players that the clubface should remain facing the target as it is swung in order for the golf ball to go straight. This is why the act of rotating the arms, right over left, needs to be emphasized before even one golf ball is hit during the very first golf lesson.

91

That Bent Left Arm On The Backswing

Trying to keep the left elbow or left arm straight often seems impossible for many beginners and again with many ladies and trying to do so just adds more tension to an already stressful experience. Many times the problem originates with the way these students were taught to start their backswing. If they were taught to start back with their left arm or to take the golf club straight back it is easy to see why the left arm would not remain extended. For a beginner, that golf club might feel like a ten pound weight by the time it reaches waist-high especially if they were told to take the golf club back "slowly." Also as they possibly were not told anything about hinging their wrists, something has to give, usually their left elbow.

Again the bent left arm on the backswing is not in itself a flaw but a symptom. If the head of the golf club is start back with the dominant right hand using a "swinging motion" and if the wrists hinge normally and gradually there will be no tension in the left arm and it will nearly always remain extended all the way to the top of the backswing.

Your Shoe May Have Been "Trained" Wrong

Many times I have observed a player "setting themselves up for failure" before they even hit a golf ball. Much of the time the things that obviously need work are the basics of grip, stance, posture, rhythm, weight movement, flexibility and so on. These fairly common things show up as soon as the student takes a practice swing. One thing shows up even sooner when I see a student walking to the lesson tee. When I notice that the student's right golf shoe exhibits a "pushed-out" to the right appearance I know I have my work cut out for me. This "shoe deformity" has been caused by many months or even years of allowing too much weight to move to the outside of the right foot on the backswing. As this movement will make it impossible to work on correct foot work there is a very good chance that this student will be unable to return adequate weight to the left foot in time to make good contact with the golf ball. More than once I have suggested that these students invest in a good pair of golf shoes before we proceed.

Sandals, Really!

It has been reported that Sam Snead often practiced barefoot. The only thing I could comment on about this would be that he must have had a very strong right big toe or very flexible ankles that would allow him to finish with most of his weight on his left foot. The folks I attempt to teach that show up wearing sandals don't seem to have Snead's strong toe or flexible ankles and have little or no chance of finishing on their left foot with a full golf swing. This is another instance where I recommend a pair of real golf shoes.

If It Aint Broke, Don't Try To Change It

Too often I have seen a young player with a good golf swing become frustrated and disillusioned with their golf game after some well-meaning young teacher has tried to change their golf swing to conform to what the teacher envisions as "correct." What many instructors fail to realize is that most players develop "their" golf swing shortly after first being introduced to the game and most players should be encouraged to work with the golf swing they have and as long as there are no serious errors.

It is seldom productive to attempt to have a senior or any golfer who has been playing the game for a number of years make any drastic change in the way they swing the golf club. Grip, stance, alignment, better finish position and timing can often be improved but things like "swing plane" or position of the golf club at the top of the backswing just are not likely to change regardless of what the instructor feels might be better.

Correcting Those Errant Golf Shots

All of us have experienced a slice, pull, duck hook, topped shot, fat shot, shank or even a "whiff." When a good player hits an errant golf shot they know or should know immediately what caused it and likely will not repeat that same mistake again during that   round. They may over-compensate for the mistake when faced with a similar situation but will seldom make the same mistake over again.

The average player is very likely to repeat their mistake that caused a bad golf shot because they were unsure of what caused the problem. They will immediately start having doubts about their golf swing and start trying various changes which usually just add to the confusion. This player would be better off just trying to regain their lost tempo and make no basic changes in their golf swing until they are able to get to the practice tee.

Once the basics outlined in this book have been learned and put into play and the concept of the "swinging motion" of the golf club has been understood many of the poorly hit golf shots will be eliminated.

It is much easier and more productive to think about that positive motion on the golf course than to think about all the wrong things that may happen.

Nevertheless, bad shots do happen and knowing just what may need to be worked on to correct a problem when it happens frequently is necessary.

There may be more ways to mess up a golf shot than I will go into here but I will try to cover most of them as well as suggest practice drills to protect against them. As I suggested before, a good teaching pro can be of great assistance.

The "Root" Cause Of The Slice, Pull, Pull-Hook And Shank

Just stating here that these four shots are caused by the same bad movement may seem an over simplification but I have found that they are very closely related.

> **If we examine the path of the club head as any of these bad shots occur we would find they were exactly the same.**

The club head has approached the golf ball from outside the intended path to the target. This is often referred as swinging "outside-in" or "coming across the ball."

When the shot is a "pull" the club head has struck the golf ball from outside the intended path with the clubface facing along the erroneous swing path.

When the shot is a "pull-hook" the swing path is the same but the clubface is facing left of the erroneous swing path.

When the shot is a "slice" the swing path is the same but the clubface was facing to the right of that erroneous swing path.

When the shot is a "shank" the swing path is basically the same but to the extreme and the clubface may have been faced to the right, left or straight.

What all these golf shots have in common is the path of the club head. It is being swung to the left of the target. The first obvious thing to check when trying to determine why the golf club is being swung to the left is alignment. Many times the player will be lined up incorrectly, especially with their shoulders and arms and this is the hoped for solution. If this solves the "outside-in" problem the position of the clubface can then be addressed.

These four fairly common problems involve making two adjustments, the "outside-in" movement and the position of the clubface.

If the clubface problem is corrected first through a possible grip change or working on the rotation of the arms the curve of the golf ball will be different but the golf ball will still start left of the target line. If the problem of swinging from "outside-in" is addressed by having the student practice hitting through "goal posts" or over an interim target the ball will gradually begin to start down the target line but may still curve right or left.

Unfortunately, in this situation, both corrections will need to be worked on at the same time and very few students have the patience or will devote adequate time to making these very obvious and much needed corrections. For those who do really want to improve I would suggest the "goal post" drill described in the chapter on the downswing as well as some serious work with a Teaching Professional on any needed grip changes. Anyone thinking they will correct these problems by taking a one-hour golf lesson is dreaming. These changes will take many hours of help plus many hours of practice to have any chance of improvement. On top of that there should be no play on the golf course without an instructor and absolutely no listening to suggestions from anyone else including but not limited to a spouse, playing buddy or priest.

Correcting The Push

Show me a player who hits their golf ball to the right of their target with little or no curve and I will show you a player who is very close to hitting a good golf shot. I feel that a push is what might be described as too much of a good thing. At least this shot is not "over-the-top." Most players who experience hitting a push either swing their golf club too much inside their line on their backswing or allow their body to get too much ahead of their arms and golf club on their downswing. As this is very rare shot with the average player I would offer no suggestions other than to check the path of the golf club on the backswing, keep the body still longer on the downswing and use the "goal post" drill until the golf ball can be started toward the center of the posts consistently.

"Topped," "Thin" And "Fat" Golf Shots

Many times the "thin" shot and "topped" shot are the result of not watching the spot where the golf ball was sitting long enough. As the eyes play a big part in controlling where the club head is as it approaches the golf ball on the downswing, letting the eyes or head start to move before the golf ball is contacted will usually effect where the bottom of the stroke actually is. You can demonstrate this to yourself by looking three or four inches ahead of the golf ball as you attempt to hit it. You will find that you will "top" the golf ball nearly every time or possibly miss it altogether. Just watching the spot where your golf ball was sitting until you feel your right arm swing past your chin as you practice is the best drill I know of to help solve this problem.

If not watching the ball long enough is not a problem and the player experiences "fat" golf shots as well as the two above the problem is nearly always that the player's weight has remained on the right foot (back foot) too long or possibly has not ever moved adequately to the left foot (front foot). Many times the problem originated with a "sway" back to the right foot making it impossible to get the weight onto the left foot in time. The various reasons for not having enough weight going to the left foot (front foot) need to be discovered and may be vastly different for each player. Again, this correction can probably not be made without the help of an instructor and will involve many hours of practice before trying to take the corrected golf swing to the golf course.

Student And Teacher Must Communicate

As many hours of good golf swings are televised each week along with slow motion of the top players you would think that everyone in the world would know that the club head should strike the golf ball with a downward stroke, taking the divot well after hitting the golf ball. I am always amazed when working with students that many believe the bottom of the arc should be beneath the golf ball or even behind it in order to get the golf ball airborne. I can't help but wonder where they have been, whether they still believe the world is flat or what TV they have been watching. How can an instructor expect a student to make a correction if they are not even envisioning the same golf swing?

Correcting a flaw in a golf swing that has been well ingrained in a student's golf swing for a long period of time is seldom an easy job and may involve using many different ways of saying the same thing before something clicks. Correcting a flaw also may involve some experimenting with different ideas or even tricks to fool the student's body into performing differently. I recently suggested to a student who was having trouble correcting an "outside-in" move to try to hit their right foot with the golf club as they started their downswing. The first move down was greatly improved and they never did actually hit their right foot so for this student a somewhat weird thought actually did help. I had suggested the same correction to another student a year or so ago but never heard from him again so I presume it either didn't work or he broke a bone in his foot and quit the game.

Learning to swing a golf club well enough to enjoy the game and being able and willing to make a needed correction in a golf swing does not come easy or quickly but can be done with correct supervision, a lot of practice, knowledge about the golf swing, a lot of determination and sometimes a little experimenting.

Part Two

The Short Game

Chapter Eight

The Scoring Shots
The Importance Of The Short Game

I know that everyone who has ever starting trying to learn the game of golf has been told countless times that the putter, chipping clubs and wedges were the most important golf clubs in their golf bag. In spite of this very few players of any ability spend nearly enough time learning or practicing those vital golf shots from on or near the putting surface.

In general I would consider a "short game" shot to be anything from the cup out to about fifty yards. Beyond fifty yards or so the golf swing normally would be rather full and the same suggestions as those covered under the chapters on the full golf swing would apply. The argument could be made that the driver is the most important golf club in a player's golf bag and I would not disagree entirely, as the golf game becomes a lot easier if the golf ball ends up long and straight down the fairway. The problem is that the average player seems to spend much more time practicing their tee shot which, unless playing an intentional draw or fade, involves using just one type of golf swing about fourteen times in a round of golf.

The variety of swings which might be used from fifty yards or less from the putting surface may involve fifteen or so different types of golf strokes with a half dozen or so different golf clubs. For example, a 56 degree sand wedge could be used for a chip shot, a lob shot, a "gravity" shot, a pitch shot, four or five different bunker shots, a "belly" shot from the fringe or even a putt. The sand wedge might be considered the most versatile golf club in a player's bag. It would seem logical then that players should practice their various "short game" clubs many times more than they practice their tee shots.

Very few players have enough different "short game" golf shots in their arsenal to score well on those days their long shots are less than perfect.

Entire books have been written on those important golf shots near the green and there are numerous instructors who specialize only on teaching those golf shots so I have just touched on the basics in this chapter. As the short pitch shots are more closely related to full swing shots I have covered in preceding chapters I will commence with these and then work in toward the cup.

What golf club to use and what type of golf shot to attempt from fifty yards out or even closer to the putting surface is not an exact science and would depend on factors such as the hardness of the putting surface, thickness of the turf under the golf ball, weather conditions, understanding the characteristics of different golf clubs and the confidence in the shot being considered.

The first step would be to learn the mechanics involved in a variety of golf shots using different golf clubs then practice enough to have some degree of confidence in those golf shots before trying to use them under pressure.

There is no absolute or consistent correlation between how long your backswing should be, how much wrist hinge is needed or how much power to apply for a certain distance or condition. Expertise can only be achieved by understanding the basics as they apply to various golf shots, adapting those basics to your own limitations and abilities and practicing until you have enough confidence to take them to the golf course. Generally the shorter the golf shot the more mechanical the golf swing will be but in the end it all comes down to "feel." A six-inch putt, for example would be about 99% mechanics whereas a thirty-yard pitch shot from a poor lie would involve both mechanics and feel. Mechanics you can learn rather easily and are mostly logical but feel can only come from practice.

What Do You Call Those Golf Shots?

First in order of importance is to become familiar with the terms you hear when referring to the many short game golf shots then continue with a description of the mechanics involved in hitting these shots. I will try to avoid using the common terms you might hear on the golf course after these shots have been miss-hit.

Pitch Shot: Generally a lofted shot hit with wedges having lofts from about 52 degrees to 64 degrees. The greater the loft the higher the golf shot can be hit. The greater the "bounce" or the bump on the bottom of the golf club the less it will dig into the turf or sand. Loft can be increased by opening the face of the golf club at address.

Pitch and Run and Chip Shot: When we think of a pitch shot we normally are thinking about a lofted wedge shot where the golf ball will stop rather quickly when it lands on the putting surface. There are instances however when we do not need much loft or to have the golf ball stop quickly. In these circumstances there is no need to use a wedge with high loft or to open the clubface at address. As a chip shot involves the same fundamentals I have included it here.

Bump and Run: This term is used to describe a shot which lands just short of the putting surface and hopefully continues on toward the flagstick. This golf shot may be hit with a number of clubs generally with less loft than a wedge as no backspin is needed.

Flop Shot: Of all the different type of golf shots near the putting surface this shot requires the most practice and most confidence. This short golf shot which is intended to fly high and land softly on the putting surface has been a trademark of Phil Mickelson.

The Recovery Shot from High Grass: A lot has been written and shown on T-V about taking a very long backswing when hitting a golf ball from a lie in high grass near the putting surface. This golf shot most amateurs are reluctant to use but a great tool to have.

Hinge and Hold: An important technique also made famous by Phil Mickelson may be used anywhere from just a few inches off the putting surface, in a bunker or from further out.

Various Bunker (Sand Trap) Shots: Whether you refer to them as "bunkers" or "sand traps" these golf shots seem to cause the most fear and difficulty for the average player. I will attempt to cover a range of golf shots which may be encountered but as with most of the "scoring shots" any degree of proficiency will depend on the time spent practicing these shots.

Putting Basics: I always tell my students that putting is more of an "individual" thing than any other golf shot. With the recently enacted rules regarding "anchoring" the golf club against any part of the body, some of these choices may be taken away. Regardless of rule changes certain basics still apply with any putter or putting stroke.

Reading the Green: Some golfers seem to have little difficulty determining the speed of a green or the direction of the break while others just never seem to get it right. Again I will attempt to cover the most agreed upon basics but there is no substitute for experience and local knowledge with this critical part of the golf game.

Using The Wedges And Chipping Clubs

A normal pitch shot would include any golf shot from a normal lie, under normal conditions being hit with any lofted golf club with the intent of having the golf ball land softly on the putting surface. A full swing with a pitching wedge from 130 yards or so or a lob wedge with a ¾ swing from 40 yards or so out could both be called pitch shots and the fundamentals involved would be very similar.

Wrist Hinge: A pitch shot would require a rather full wrist hinge on the backswing, as much shoulder turn as necessary for the distance the shot needs to be hit and very little movement of the lower body.

Judging Distance: Distance is governed by the length of the backswing, the loft of the golf club being used and the speed of the downswing. The feeling I like to have my students work toward on the short shots is that the speed of the backswing and the speed of the downswing are about the same. The average player tends to take the club back much too short on the backswing and accelerate too much on the downswing. I tell my students to let the backswing determine the distance. Tempo is critical on all pitch shots as the goal is accuracy not distance.

Stance: I recommend an "open" and rather narrow stance for short shots mainly to limit the length of the backswing. This position also makes it a little easier to aim toward the target and to leave the clubface open when necessary.

The Open Clubface: Experienced players add loft and backspin by opening the clubface at address. Most beginners have a difficult time adjusting to the look of the open clubface as it would appear that the golf ball would fly to the right. A rule of thumb would be that the golf ball will start about half way between where the clubface is faced and the direction of the swing. The open clubface will affect height more than direction but this idea will take a lot of getting used to for the average beginner or even a more advanced player who has not practiced the shot.

The new more lofted wedges take a little less talent to hit those lofted shots but caution must be used when trying to open the face of a 60 or 64 degree wedge from long grass as it is very easy to have the club head slide completely under the golf ball.

Bounce: Modern wedges are not only designed with various degrees of loft but also with different "bounces" on the bottom of the club head. The greater the protruding bump on the bottom of the golf club the less it will tend to dig into the turf or sand. When hitting from a normal grassy lie in the fairway this would not be a problem but when the golf ball is sitting on very shortly mowed grass or bare dirt the "bounce" may cause the club head to hit the center of the golf ball resulting in a "skulled" shot. When a wedge with "bounce" is addressed with an open clubface the "bounce" becomes greater and the golf shot more difficult from a less than perfect lie. The higher loft wedges will normally have less "bounce" and will enable the player to get loft without having to open the clubface to an extreme. My best advice would be to get to know your wedges, make the loft and "bounce" on those golf clubs work for you and don't try to hit a golf shot the golf club wasn't designed to hit.

Backspin: Backspin is caused by the club striking the golf ball with a descending blow. The loft of the clubface, the groves and speed of the club head all contribute to the amount of backspin. Most amateurs do not hit golf shots with enough of a downward stroke and speed to see their golf ball spin back toward them when it lands on the putting surface. Many of the top players on the PGA Tour find themselves having to swing with less power to avoid having too much spin. For the rest of us just having enough backspin to keep our golf ball from running over the green into a back bunker should be enough to make us happy.

Pitch And Run or "Chip" Shot

Definitions: One of the easiest approach shots to learn and probably the one in which the average player has the most confidence can be used very effectively when there is no obstacle to hit over and there is quite a bit of putting surface between the edge of the green and the flagstick. We often refer to a shot from just off the putting surface with a lofted club as a "pitch and run" and the same shot using a less lofted golf club as a "chip." As both these golf shots are hit using the same fundamentals I will treat them the same. When asked by my students what the difference is between a pitch shot and a chip, I usually just reply that the pitch is a high shot and the chip is a low shot although I realize this is an over-simplification.

Where to Land the Golf Ball: There are two schools of thought about how far onto the putting surface a golf ball should carry. One idea is to get the golf ball on the putting surface as soon as possible. The other idea is to fly the golf ball as near the cup as possible. Getting the golf ball on the putting surface as soon as possible involves more reading of the green whereas carrying the golf ball further depends a lot on the first bounce and any backspin put on the golf ball. I cannot say which is the better of the two ideas as every lie, slope and speed of the putting surface are different. It all comes down to how confident the player is in the shot selected.

Address Basics: There are three basic fundamental rules for hitting a chip or pitch and run.

1. Keep your weight very much on your left foot. (right foot for lefties)
2. Play the golf ball back in your stance.
3. Place your hands well ahead of the club head.

Other Good Ideas at Address:

1. Keep your left hand fairly firm.
2. Do not reach too far.
3. Use an open stance.
4. Use a golf club with enough loft to carry over the fringe.

**Weight left,
ball back,
hands ahead.**

Backswing:

1. **Do not move your body**, just your arms.
2. Let the length of your backswing determine distance.
3. It is OK to hinge your wrists slightly. A hinging of the wrists will raise your club head more off the turf than a more stiff-wristed stroke such as used with a putter. This slight hinging of the wrists will help avoid a "fat" shot and promote a more downward stroke.

Alternate method: For kids or beginners with little feel of their club head, a putting stroke may be used when the golf ball rests on very short grass.

The length of backstroke determines distance.

Downswing:

1. Keep your hands ahead of the club head.
2. Use a slightly downward stroke.
3. Use the weight of the club head and the length of the backswing for distance control.
4. Avoid any rapid acceleration.

The Finish:

1. See that your hands are still ahead of the club head.
2. See that most of your weight is still on the left foot.
3. Never force a "follow-through." The turf may stop your club head, especially in higher grass.

After contact with the ball the hands are still ahead of the club head.

Club Selection:

You should resist the idea of having a favorite golf club for these short golf shots and work on learning how far various golf clubs carry your golf ball onto the putting surface. You should also keep in mind that a lofted club such as a wedge will always have some backspin when struck with a descending club head and allow for this when picking a golf club.

Most Common Mistakes:

1. Keeping the weight too much on the right (back) foot.
2. Playing the golf ball too much forward in the stance.
3. Hands were not far enough ahead of the club head.
4. Backswing too short for the distance needed.
5. Too much acceleration on the forward stroke.

6. Trying to "loft" the golf ball rather than hitting down and letting the loft of the golf club determine height.
7. Using the wrong golf club for the situation.
8. Not enough practice.

The Bump and Run

The fundamentals for the bump and run are about the same as those for a pitch and run described above. The main difference is that this golf shot is used when it may be necessary to land the golf ball a little short of the putting surface allowing it to bounce one or more times before reaching that putting surface. Experience and experimentation are the best teachers when learning when to use or not use this shot and what golf club should be used. With experience it is possible to visualize what the golf ball would probably do prior to choosing a golf club.

A bump and run shot can be used anywhere from just a few feet off the putting surface or out several yards when a low, running golf shot is called for or when there is just no other golf shot that would work. The player sometimes needs to calculate the odds against using a lofted pitch shot or low running bump and run.

To practice this very useful golf shot I would suggest imagining that you are chipping then ask yourself what would be different if you needed to hit the same low, running shot twenty yards or so. You would find these similarities:

1. You still need to play the golf ball back in your stance.
2. You still to keep your hands ahead of your club head at address and at contact.
3. You still need to hit the shot with a descending stroke.

4. As you generally have further to go, you will need more wrist hinge on the backswing.
5. You still don't need any weight shift back to the right foot.
6. Distance you need to hit the golf shot is still determined mainly by the length of the backswing.
7. You still must not force a "follow-through."
8. You still need to practice with different golf clubs.
9. You still must learn to visualize the shot before you even pick a golf club for the shot.

The Flop Shot

The flop shot is used when there is a need to get the golf ball in the air quickly and have it land softly on the putting surface. There is not a lot of backspin expected on this golf shot as it is not hit with much club head speed. What the player hopes for is that the height of the golf ball will prevent it from running very far when it lands on the putting surface. Before 60° and 64° wedges came along it was necessary to lay the face of sand wedge very much open to have any chance of hitting the golf ball with the tremendous amount of loft that is seen today with the high lofted wedges. This improvement in golf club design has resulted in more golfers being able to execute golf shots which before had been nearly impossible.

One thing which should be pointed out is that the high lofted wedges do not have as much bounce on the sole of the club head as the normal sand wedge. When a wedge with a large bounce is laid open there is a good possibility that the leading edge of the club head will not be able to contact the bottom of the golf ball unless the golf ball is setting up well in the grass. With the more lofted wedges there usually is no need to open the clubface to any extent to get the needed loft on the golf ball so the lob shot becomes a much easier golf shot to hit.

As with any other golf shot there are certain fundamentals which when followed will make this lob shot easier to execute:

1. Use the most lofted golf club in your golf bag.
2. Never use a wedge with much bounce unless your golf ball is resting on fairly thick grass.
3. Play your golf ball in the center or more toward your left foot at address unless your golf ball is on dirt or very short turf.
4. Take a fairly full backswing, depending on the distance you would like your golf ball to travel.
5. You do not need to lean on your left foot as you would for other short wedge shots but still must avoid any movement of your weight back to your right foot.
6. Avoid any attempt to help your golf ball get in the air quickly. Let your golf club take care of this.
7. When hitting a lob shot from deeper grass, it will be impossible to hit the golf ball before making contact with the turf. In this case the shot would be played more like a bunker shot as the club head would need to enter the grass a few inches in back of the golf ball. Do not expect much of a finish when hitting through higher grass.
8. These high shots should be practiced using a lob wedge or a sand wedge but every player has their favorite way of playing these shots. They cannot be learned from reading a book but hopefully the fundamentals learned here will give the serious student a little head start for their practice sessions.

The Hinge And Hold Technique

I feel that the "hinge and hold" technique as demonstrated so well on TV by Phil Mickelson is one of the most necessary movements of the "short game." This is not a different golf shot but rather a way of hitting many short golf shots including the chip shot, pitch and run and other wedge shots requiring accuracy and touch. In the description of how to hit a chip shot I emphasized that it is necessary to hinge the wrists on the backswing but keep the hands leading the club head on the downswing. This is exactly what is meant by "hinge and hold" and that same technique can and should be used anywhere from the fringe of the green to as far out as the individual player can become comfortable using it.

In the photos, I demonstrate the positions the player and the club head should be in at various stages of the swing using this technique. Another way of expressing the way this method might feel would be, cock the wrists a little but don't uncock them through the hitting area and finish. For me, I feel that I need to tighten my grip on the golf club, keep my wrists extra firm as I start the golf club down and keep my weight very much on my left foot throughout the entire swing. As the wrists hinge on the backswing the club head naturally swings open through the downswing giving the golf ball a little extra loft. Also, as the golf ball is being contacted using a downward stroke with an open clubface there is normally some backspin.

The centrifugal force which is so necessary to supply power and allow the clubface to close through the impact area, with all other golf shots, must be tightly controlled when using this very precise technique. If you find that your club head has passed your hands at the finish of this stroke, you are not hitting it correctly. You must pull your hands as one unit, still hinged, through contact with the golf ball.

115

Showing hinge and hold technique.

The Recovery Shot from High Grass

Occasionally you may find your golf ball nestled in very high grass when it should be obvious that hitting the golf ball without first plowing through a lot of grass would be impossible. It would also not be possible to use the long, low stroke you would like, have any finish or get any backspin at all on the golf ball. The four most important things you need in this circumstance are loft, power, gravity and humility. One thing you likely are not going to get out of this kind of lie is distance so hopefully you don't need to go very far. This shot has been called the "gravity shot" as it is hit using the heaviest golf club in your golf bag "dropped" from as high as possible behind the golf ball.

As the sand wedge is the golf club with the heaviest head it would be the golf club most likely to get your golf ball out of this situation. The stroke or "chop" should be hit as follows:

1. Use a wide stance for stability.
2. Do not open the clubface much or the "bounce" of the club head may not penetrate the thick grass.
3. Play the golf ball about in the center of your stance or even further toward your front foot about the same as you would do in a bunker.
4. Keep your weight mostly on your left foot to assure a downward stroke.
5. Pick up the club head abruptly with your hands and wrists to avoid getting tangled in the high grass behind the golf ball.
6. Swing as high and long on your backswing as possible to put as much gravity as possible into the shot.
7. Swing down and fairly hard a few inches back of the golf ball.
8. Use a very firm grip as the grass will cause the club head to close when the grass wraps around the shaft of the golf club.

9. You should allow for the golf ball flying left of your target when hitting from any high grass lie.
10. Do not attempt to "finish" or "follow through."
11. Don't try for a miracle shot. Just get the ball back into play.

Bunker Shots (Sand Traps)

Many of my older readers might remember that what we now hear referred to as a "bunker" used to be called a "sand trap." Sometimes when the golf course couldn't afford to maintain a "sand trap" or too many members complained about its location, the greens keeper threw a little dirt into the depression and let the grass grow longer than the normal rough. It then became a "grass bunker" but we still had "sand traps." Now if you tell a young pro that you were in a "sand trap" he will look at you as if you had just written down the wrong score. Whatever you want to call it the following pages might give you a few ideas on how to best get your golf ball out of that big hole full of sand with rakes lying around it.

Normal Club Selection and Technique: Just because you probably have a sand wedge you don't necessarily have to use that golf club every time you find your golf ball in sand. As shown earlier, your sand wedge probably has a big "bounce" on the bottom which will help prevent your club head from digging too deeply onto the sand. From normal, well raked and fairly dry sand you may want to open the clubface quite a bit when you need a little extra loft on your golf shot and don't need a lot of distance.

From this fairly fluffy lie you should be able to have your golf club enter the sand four or five inches behind the golf ball and slide under the ball without swinging very hard. This would be the ideal bunker lie and one we would hope for every time. As you are trying to have your club head enter the sand fairly far behind the golf ball you should not expect very much backspin however this will be the safest way to be sure you are at least on the putting surface and using a putter for your next shot. You should practice these basics for a normal bunker shot.

Address Position:

1. Your weight should be very much on your left (front) foot. Feel as though you are leaning left.
2. Dig your feet in to avoid slipping.
3. If in normal sand from a flat lie you may open your clubface as much as is comfortable for you.
4. Play the golf ball a little ahead of center or toward your left foot.
5. Focus on the spot you would like the club head to enter the sand.
6. Open your stance.

It is critical to keep your lower body very still on the backswing on all bunker shots.

Backswing:

1. Cock your wrists as early as possible.
2. Keep your weight just as it was at address.
3. Take as long a backswing as needed for the distance needed.
4. Keep your lower body very still.

Downswing:

1. Watch your club head enter the sand at the spot you have picked.
2. For most players the feeling would be that you are "splashing" the sand with your right hand in control.
3. You will need to swing hard enough so the sand does not stop your club head.

Watch the head of the golf club splash the sand behind the golf ball.

The Finish:

1. Your weight should be still very much on your left foot.

2. Your right arm may have rotated over your left just as in any other golf swing unless you are purposely trying to hold your clubface open for additional loft on the golf ball.

3. Your focus should be on the spot you were trying to have your golf club enter the sand well into your finish.

Now you can admire your golf shot.

Using a Different Wedge: Additional distance can be achieved by using a "gap" wedge or pitching wedge. As both of these golf clubs have less bounce they will tend to dig deeper into the sand so you would normally need to have your club head enter the sand closer to the golf ball than when using a sand wedge. They will also come out of the bunker much lower they are not best for many greenside bunker shots. This is one of those golf shots rarely used but good to know.

The high lofted wedges are very helpful in two different situations. One would be if additional height is needed without opening the clubface when your golf ball is in firmer sand and you do not want your golf club to bounce. As these clubs have less flange or "bounce" they will tend to dig in too deeply if your club head enters the sand very far behind the golf ball.

The other situation would be when you need to get your golf ball to fly very high as is the case when the flagstick is close to the bunker. When you are playing from normal sand you would want to address the golf ball with your clubface open much more than normal. When you do this you will increase the amount of "bounce" on the club head. This "bounce" will prevent your club head from digging into the sand too much. There is less room for error with these wedges than with a regular sand wedge but they can be great tools with a little practice.

Getting the Ball to Stop: There are only two ways to get your golf ball to stop when playing from a bunker. One is by hitting the shot as high as possible using a very lofted wedge, opening the clubface as much as possible or a combination of these. The second and most difficult method is to put as much backspin on the shot as possible by hitting as close to the golf ball as you have the nerve to do.

Just as when playing from high grass, the more sand your club head has to plow through behind your golf ball the less backspin you will have. Conversely, the less sand you contact behind your golf ball the more backspin you ball will have. The problem is that the average golfer just does not have the ability to be able to have their golf club head enter the sand one or two inches behind their golf ball as would be required for backspin. Any player can, with enough practice, learn to hit this shot but it will remain one of the most difficult and dangerous golf shots to attempt.

The goal of most of us should first be just being able to get our golf ball on the putting surface. Focusing on a spot five inches or so behind the golf ball and missing the spot that spot an inch or so will usually not be disastrous and will still get the golf ball out of the bunker and somewhere on the putting surface. Missing that spot even an inch when trying to have your golf club enter the sand two inches behind the golf ball has ruined the day for many players. Sure, we can pull off that "miracle" shot occasionally but it is sometimes better to ask ourselves what the odds are against trying a golf shot we have not really practiced enough or at all.

Embedded Ball, Wet Sand, Packed Sand or Mud: There are several times when you can throw all the ideas about letting your golf club do the work, finishing correctly or swinging smoothly out the window. There are still some common sense principals that need to be considered, however, when we find ourselves facing difficult lies in a bunker. There are two different ways we want our golf club to enter the sand in a bunker. We either want our wedge to penetrate or dig downward into the sand or we want our golf club to merely brush under our golf ball. All of the bunker shots discussed previously would apply when our golf ball rests in normal or "fluffy" sand in a greenside bunker and we wanted to use a "sweeping" action with the golf club.

There are many times when the most important consideration would be how to slide the golf club get under the golf ball without the club head "bouncing" into the center of the golf ball. In these instances we will need to forget any idea of "sweeping" the golf club under the golf ball. We now will need to "dig" into the sand behind the golf ball. If we were to think about the "bounce" on the bottom of the sand wedge as opposed to the leading edge of that club or even that of a lob wedge it should be obvious that we cannot "dig" with a part of the wedge that is designed to "bounce." By closing the head of the sand wedge the sharp leading edge will be able to enter the sand and "dig" deeper than if the bounce of that golf club enters the sand first.

At Address:

1. Take a wide stance.
2. Grip the golf club firmly.
3. Lean on your left foot.
4. Close the clubface.
5. Have your hands well ahead.
6. Focus on a spot well behind the golf ball.

Backswing:

1. Pick the club head up rather steeply.
2. Keep you lower body still
3. Be sure your wrists hinge fully.
4. Don't be afraid to swing long for power.

Downswing:

1. Try to "bury" your club head behind the golf ball.
2. Use your right hand for power.
3. Swing fairly hard.
4. Keep your weight moving to your left foot.

The Finish:

1. Do not force a finish. The sand may cause your club head to stop.

2. Your weight should be very much on your left foot.

    If you are in a "fried egg" lie, be sure to have your golf club enter the sand behind the whole indentation.

Under the Lip: What may seem to be an impossible lie may actually be the most simple if the following simple rules are followed.

At Address:

1. As it will be impossible to put your weight on your left foot, lean as much left as possible and brace your right leg.
2. Generally you will need to open your clubface to get the needed height
3. Focus on a spot far enough behind the golf ball to prevent striking the golf ball with the club head.

Lean on the left foot as much as possible.

Try to bury the club head in the sand.

The Swing:

1. Your focus and goal is to try to "bury" your club head in the sand under the golf ball.
2. Take as full a swing with your arms and hands as possible.
3. Swing hard.
4. You will have no finish at all as the bank or lip of the bunker will stop your club head.

The Downhill Lie In a Bunker: I can think of no other shot in golf that is more difficult or which causes the most problems for golfers of any ability. Few players practice this shot but most should. In an extreme downhill lie it is sometimes best to just hit the golf ball out of the bunker toward a better position rather than attempting the nearly impossible task of trying to hit the golf ball onto the putting surface. There are certain basics which will apply when facing these shots.

At Address:

1. Take as wide a stance as possible.
2. Lean very much on the left foot.
3. Close the clubface with a sand wedge or use a more lofted wedge also with a closed clubface.
4. Play the golf ball back in the stance.
5. Grip the golf club very firmly.

The Swing:

1. Pick the club head up very abruptly with the right hand in control.
2. Keep your weight very much on your left leg.
3. Try to "bury" the club head behind the golf ball.
4. Do not expect a "finish."

Putting Basics

For the sake of learning, putting must be divided into two parts:

1. The **direction** you want your golf ball to go and
2. The **speed** of the golf ball.

Direction is determined by two factors:

1. The direction your club head is traveling at contact with your golf ball.
2. How much that direction may be altered by terrain, weather factors and peculiarities in the putting surface.

*Direction may also be affected by the position of the clubface (open or closed) at contact with the golf ball but this seldom is a problem if the clubface is lined up correctly at address.

The speed of your golf ball, when putting, is determined by:
1. How fast your club head is traveling when it contacts the golf ball
2. How it is affected by the same terrain, weather conditions and peculiarities of the putting surface that influence direction.

Before getting into the various outside factors that affect the speed and direction of the golf ball on the putting surface it is necessary to master that part of speed and direction which can be controlled by the player through proper grip, alignment and tempo. When these factors are learned, practiced and put into play the player will be better prepared for the outside factors which can affect even a well-stroked putt.

The putting stroke can be controlled; outside factors cannot be controlled but can be recognized and allowed for.

Putting is the most individual part of the golf game so about all an instructor can do is to teach students the most logical approaches that have the best chance of success and then let the student improvise from there. There is no right or wrong way to grip the putter, what kind of putter to use or how to stroke the golf ball. All I can suggest is to try my way first and improvise when I'm not watching.

Popular Grips Using a Standard Length Putter

1. Reverse overlap: Back of left hand and palm of the right hand facing the target with both thumbs on top of the grip. The most widely accepted grip for many years. The left index finger overlaps the fingers of the right hand.

2. Left hand low: Having the left hand lower than the right tends to take some of the right hand out of the stroke resulting in a firmer stroke with the arms and involving no wrist break.

3. Palms together: A variation of the above methods usually used with an over-sized grip. This method provides a very light grip and encourages an all-arms stroke.

4. "Claw" grip: The right hand is considerably lower than the left and very much on top of the grip. This grip seems to be very effective in taking all hand or wrist breakdown out of the equation but retaining the feel that the right arm and hand are in control.

Normal Golf Ball Position: For a normal putter, playing the golf ball slightly forward in the stance with the weight somewhat on the left foot seems to make it easier to "see" the line, not hit behind the golf ball and allow the left hand to lead the stroke toward the target. The golf ball should also be placed as near as possible to the feet to allow the dominant eye to be directly over the golf ball.

The Stroke: The best putters seem to avoid any deceleration of the club as it strikes the golf ball while also avoiding any sudden acceleration. I like to have my students keep the length as well as the speed of the backswing and forward swing about the same. By watching the head of the putter swing back and through in a pendulum motion with no wrist hinge there seems to be less chance of "yipping" the putt.

Reading the Green: Only after the student has developed a smooth and efficient putting stroke on a level putting surface should deviations in the green be addressed. Those deviations involve how closely the grass has been mowed, the firmness of the surface, whether the golf ball must travel uphill or downhill, direction the grass is growing, how dry or wet the grass is, the topography of the surrounding area and even the wind.

Uphill, downhill or side hill: It is usually fairly obvious when a putt must travel up a hill or down a hill but if it is not I suggest walking from the golf ball to the cup and back to help get a feeling of whether there is a hill there or not.

Firmness of the putting surface: Again, I would suggest walking to the cup and back to try to get a feel of how firm the surface is. This becomes more of an art than mechanics and could only be learned from experience.

Length of the grass: Unless you know the greens keeper, you likely will not know the exact height the mowers were set so you are going to have to again go by experience.

Direction the grass is growing: Logic should tell you that your golf ball will travel faster if it is rolling in the direction the grass is laying. The best method of determining the "grain" when looking at the putting surface is to determine by looking which direction is dull looking and which is brighter or shinier. Dull means that the "grain" is growing toward you and the shinier the grass looks the faster the golf ball will roll.

Topography: There are times when the above methods may not show an obvious amount of hill or "grain" and walking around yields few clues. In many cases the golf ball on a seemingly flat putting surface will tend to roll toward a large body of water or away from a group of mountains. Here in the Coachella Valley of California many putts tend to break toward Indio or toward the Salton Sea.

Visualize the line of the putt: Some of the best putters claim that they can "see" the line they need to putt toward. What they mean is they are able to imagine the line they need to stroke the golf ball toward. I have found that most golfers do not spend nearly enough time thinking about their line before they start their putting stroke. A lot of visualization can be and should be done while other players are putting rather than waiting until it is your turn to putt. There is also no rule against watching another payers putt to help with your own putt as long as you don't stand directly behind or in front of their line.

Spot putting: Just as in bowling, it is far easier to roll a ball toward a spot three feet or so away than to aim at a spot or cup twenty or thirty feet away. After you have determined the line you want your putt to travel, look for a few blades of different colored grass a foot or two ahead of your golf ball but on your line. Then line up your putter toward that spot and picture your golf ball rolling over that spot.

Hit it past the cup: The golf ball will break most when it starts losing its speed so by trying to hit your golf ball a foot or so past the cup it will maintain enough speed to stay on line longer. Remember also that a short putt has never gone into the cup.

Alternate styles: The "long" putter was originally used mostly by older players to allow more of a "pendulum" stroke. The greatest benefit was for those players who had developed the tendency to "yip" their puts. There is no doubt that this style has allowed many older golfers to extend their golf careers. By anchoring the grip of the longer putter against the players chin it became less likely that the hands would work in opposite directions as is the case with a "yip."

The "belly" putter came along a few years later and served the same purpose for many players. The "belly" putter is anchored against the player's stomach and also prevents the top of the grip from suddenly going in a different direction than the right hand.

In 2012 the USGA and R & A voted to prohibit "anchoring" a putter against any part of the player's body and it now seems this rule change will go into effect in 2016. If only the players on the Champion's Tour were using and benefitting from the "long" and "belly" putters there probably would not have been any prohibition but when players on the regular PGA Tour starting using these putters and winning tournaments with them it got the attention of the governing bodies who decided that the use of these golf clubs was not in keeping with the spirit of the game. I personally do not agree that the alternate putters should be prohibited as I can personally attest to the fact that it is possible to "yip" a six foot with a "long" putter. However, as is usually the case with major decisions, I wasn't asked.

The "Yips"

For those of you who have not experienced the "yips" just continue doing whatever it is you are doing. If you have not experienced this malady I can only describe it as a sudden tightening of the hands while standing over a fairly short putt and a complete loss of any feeling of where the club head is or what it may do. When you are finally able to start the club head moving you have the feeling of an electrical shock or spasm of some kind shooting through your right hand which suddenly propels an eight foot putt six feet or more past the cup. This fear of then hitting the next putt even further past the cup usually results in the six foot putt traveling only about four feet. This then leaves a two foot putt, which by now you are probably hitting cross-handed, in the hope it will not end up back where you started.

This horrible affliction which can surface at any time has resulted in many players reverting to the "long" putter, "belly" putter, cross-handed putting, anchoring the handle of the putter against the left forearm and many other unorthodox looking methods which are in the process of being outlawed by the USGA. I am sure that no one who has experienced the "yips" would vote to outlaw any method which might serve as a treatment or even a cure for this affliction.

Besides using the "long" putter or "belly" putter the best ways to "tame the beast" seem to be by using one of the alternate grips described at the beginning of this chapter. The oversized putter grips also seem to help but it will be left up to the reader to do whatever it may take. My own case of the "yips" has been in remission for nearly eight years due to numerous grip changes and my best wishes go out to any readers who may still suffering.

In Conclusion

Every player has a golf swing that is unique to them and although I can't say that they have the swing they were born with this statement is not far from the truth. Golfers develop their own golf swings when they first decide to take up the game and that golf swing is formed by their physical and mental aptitude as well as the mental picture of a golf swing they develop very early in their golfing experience.

A golfer can no more change "their" golf swing than they could change the way they walk. Most people walk with their feet pointed slightly outward. Other people walk with their feet pointed straight ahead and others walk "pigeon-toed." A young "walking instructor" might tell the "pigeon-toed" walker they would need to change the direction their toes are pointed to ever be able to walk better or run faster and that individual might indeed be able to make that change on the practice track but never on a real sidewalk especially when being chased by a mugger.

As a Teaching Professional, I often encourage a student who walks with their toes slightly outward to address the golf ball with their left foot even more outward to facilitate a better turn onto the left foot. I might also encourage that student to point their right foot straighter to help prevent an excessive move back to the right foot on their backswing. I obviously would not make the same recommendations to a student who tends to walk with their toes pointed inward or even straight ahead as these changes would only cause undue stress.

Neither would I encourage a player who addresses the golf ball with a very "hunched-over" position to immediately attempt to adapt the "sway-back" position many of the top tour players have. They might look better addressing the golf ball but would be so uncomfortable they would have trouble ever making solid contact.

I realize also that many top players have a "flat" wrist position at the top of their backswings but this is a trait they either have naturally or have developed early in their training. It would be virtually impossible for a student who has had a "cupped" wrist position for many years to change to a "flat-wrist" position and do so with any consistency. The wrist joints hinge differently for each individual as they swing a golf club just as the ankle joints hinge differently for each individual when walking. These natural movements may be altered intentionally with enough practice but will always revert to what is natural under the pressure of actually playing the game.

What can be changed and improved on are the very simple things I have written about in this book but still are subject to the physical and motivational limitations of each student. These basics are grip, stance, reasonable posture, good alignment, adequate wrist hinge, arm rotation and training the various body parts to react to the swinging motion of the golf club.

There is absolutely no reason for any player to be thinking about anything on the golf course other than where they intend to hit their golf ball. All needed corrections must be worked out on the practice tee not the golf course and even those must be kept very basic to have any chance of being taken to the golf course.

"Short-game" shots are the most neglected part of most golfers' training but at the same time the most critical for improving scoring. Many of these such as chipping, bunker play and a great variety of pitch shots call for using certain proven techniques to have any chance of success. Few golfers I see on the golf course or chipping green seem to have any idea how to avoid even the most common errors. Unlike the full golf swing those "short-game" shots just have to be executed in certain ways to be successful. They are much less subject to the player's physical makeup and past training than the full golf swing and therefore much easier to teach, learn and improve on.

The bad news for many golfers is still that all golf shots need to be practiced correctly to have any chance of improvement. Learning what to practice often can only be determined with the help of a good teacher. The good news is that anyone can improve, not by changing "their" golf swing but rather by working to improve the golf swing they have.

Jack Gibson
jackg@pga.com